EPHESIANS

Breaking Down Barriers & Living Secure

A W.O.R.T.H.Y. Bible Study

Beth Steffaniak

DEDICATION

I dedicate this book to my Lord and Savior for breaking down every barrier to make me His own, and for keeping me secure in every relationship and battle of life.

CONTENTS

W.O.R.T.H.Y. METHOD

This is a Bible study method that I developed, and feel like reflects how worthy God's word is to study and apply in our lives. My hope is that the W.O.R.T.H.Y. method will allow you to either use each day's notes as a brief devotional, or serve as a guide for writing out your own insights, takeaways, prayers and applications from your time of study—referring to my notes as an added point of view afterwards.

Welcome the Lord:
Prayerfully welcome the Lord—asking Him to reveal His truth in your time of study and prayer.

"Open my eyes that I may see wonderful things in your law."
—Psalm 119:18 (NIV)

Observe what Scripture says:
Read the passage or verse aloud once—*twice is even better*. Then use *your favorite* version to write out *word-for-word* what you observe each verse says in your Bible study journal. *Just don't forgo this step!* It really hones your ability to observe exactly what has been written in Scripture—*giving you insights into the gems that are hiding in plain sight.* (I will be using the NIV in this book.)

Recognize what is noteworthy and true:
Recognize—*and if necessary, research*—the context. This means you should look at who wrote the passage, as well as what was going on for the author and his audience at the time of the writ-

ing. Then record all the details that you recognize one-by-one and word-for-word. Notice what is important, interesting, confusing, odd, and *most importantly, true.* The main purpose under this prompt is to list or write out all of the truths and truth principles you recognize.

Thought to take:

Based off of the truths gleaned above, write out what thought you want to take with you and apply in your day. Boil this down even further into a concise action statement under "*T2t.*" Write down and keep this thought where you'll see and be reminded of it during your day.

Help: Pray for God's help to apply your T2t both *now* and all day long.

Yield: Surrender yourself to God and His truths—*reflecting on and applying your T2t* all day long.

◆ ◆ ◆

1 - CALLED AND BLESSED

Week 1, Day 1—Ephesians 1:1-2

Welcome the Lord: Ask Him to reveal His truth to you as you study.

Observe what the Scripture says:
1 - *Paul, an apostle of Christ Jesus by the will of God, To God's holy people in Ephesus, the faithful in Christ Jesus:*
2 - *Grace and peace to you from God our Father and the Lord Jesus Christ.*

Recognize what is noteworthy and true:
The letter the Apostle Paul wrote to the Ephesians is very different from all the other New Testament letters. Paul wasn't trying to address problems in any one church in this letter, but was laying out the many doctrines of the Christian faith. Some say it reads like a commentary on the other Pauline letters, and has even been dubbed the *"Queen of the Epistles."* It's also important to note the context and situation in which Paul wrote this letter. He was writing from a cold, dark Roman prison cell.

In verse 1, Paul offered a fascinating and foundational fact: He was an apostle by *"the will of God."* I find this fascinating because Paul had been persecuting and overseeing the killing of Christ-followers before Jesus confronted him on the road to Damascus—*"calling" Paul into the ministry.* Obviously, if our callings were/are based on appearances or the good we do, Paul's calling would have been a huge mistake. But, thankfully, our calling is in the hands of a mysterious and incomprehensible

God. It is His goodness, *not our own*, that matters and shines more brightly through and in spite of our brokenness and sin.

Paul's greeting included calling these believers *"holy people"* or some translations say *"saints."* The Greek word for this is translated *"sacred"* or *"holy."* Therefore, both *saints* and *holy people* are apt descriptions of these Christ-followers, as well as for every believer to come after them. As an interesting side note, in a few of the ancient manuscripts a blank space was left instead of identifying the readers as *"the Ephesians."* Some believe that this letter was written with the intention of being circulated among all the churches at that time, and was not directed *only* to the Ephesian believers.

Along with Paul's reference to the holiness of these believers, he also affirmed their *"faithfulness"* in Christ. Of course, both then and now, the holiness and faithfulness any Christ-follower can and does demonstrate was and is achieved only through Christ's power. However, I appreciate how Paul was always so quick to affirm the people whenever he wrote his letters to the churches.

In verse 2, Paul used the customary greeting in that day —*"grace and peace"*—to open his letter. However, there's an even greater significance to *"grace and peace"* as Christ-followers. First of all, the order of these two blessings from God is significant. God first extends *grace* to us at the point of our salvation and onward. God then provides *peace* in our hearts—following the grace we have embraced. I also notice that both *"God our Father"* and the *"Lord Jesus Christ"* are mentioned specifically and individually. They both provide grace and peace, yet each gives these gifts from different relational positions in our lives. One gives as our loving adopted Father, and One gives as our preeminent Lord and Savior. *I see this as the Father and Son surrounding us in grace and peace!*

Thought to take: *(Come up with one, or choose from below.)*
One clear thought to take away from this passage is how won-

derful it is to be *called by God*, no matter who I am or what I have done, as a Christ-follower. This doesn't mean every Christ-follower needs to be in vocational ministry; but we all, as fully devoted followers of Christ, must serve the Lord in whatever way we can each day. I want to embrace my calling from God and prayerfully consider what He wants me to do with each opportunity He provides for serving Him and others in my day.

T2t: *(Boil down to a brief thought, or choose from below.)*
Embrace and live out God's calling

Help: Pray for God's help to apply your T2t both now and all day long.

Father, just like the Apostle Paul, You have called me and every Christ-follower to be Your servants of the gospel—ministering by Your sovereign will and strength. You chose and knew me before I was born by preparing me to do certain good works in my lifetime. May I be faithful to You in those good works, purposes and plans. Create opportunities for me to serve You and others in my day—giving Christ the glory as a result. Then draw others to Your amazing grace through my example. I thank You for being a God who gives so richly in every possible way. Your grace and peace are lavished upon me, not just at the point of my salvation, but also in every single day of my life. And when I feel like grace and peace are elusive, may I turn my eyes back to You—the ever-present Grace-Giver and Peace-Maker in my life! In Jesus' name, amen.

Yield: Surrender yourself to God and His truths—reflecting on and applying your T2t all day long.

2 - SHOWERED IN HEAVENLY BLESSINGS

Week 1, Day 2—Ephesians 1:3-6

Welcome the Lord: Ask Him to reveal His truth to you as you study.

Observe what the Scripture says:
3 - Praise be to the God and Father of our Lord Jesus Christ, who has blessed us in the heavenly realms with every spiritual blessing in Christ.
4 - For he chose us in him before the creation of the world to be holy and blameless in his sight. In love
5 - he predestined us for adoption to sonship through Jesus Christ in accordance with his pleasure and will—
6 - to the praise of his glorious grace, which he has freely given us in the One he loves.

Recognize what is noteworthy and true:
Immediately, verse 3 reminds me that it was the same man who sat chained to a Roman guard in prison, who also spoke glowingly of his fellow-believers (v. 2), and boldly proclaimed praises of his Lord *(here in verse 3 and onward)*. Paul felt *"blessed"* and reminded us that, as Christ-followers, we are all blessed *"in the heavenly realms with every spiritual blessing in Christ."* I'm greatly encouraged by the fact that I lack no spiritual and eternal blessing in this present moment. I have everything I could ever want or need in terms of eternal blessings (2 Peter 1:3).

After all, these kinds of blessings are far higher and better than any earthly or temporary blessing. I'm sure that Paul took great comfort in this truth, since his earthly plight, at the moment of this writing, was a very bleak and threatening one.

In verse 4, Paul imparted a profound truth when he declared that God was the One to choose His own and not the other way around. The Lord did this choosing before the world was ever created—*before we ever did anything to deserve such a grand and costly gift.* And God's will in the choosing was and is that believers would be *"holy and blameless"* in His sight. I never need to worry about being holy or blameless enough for the Lord, since it is His redemption that ensures this reality.

I'm not quite sure why the words *"In love"* were placed in verse 4, rather than joining them with the thought expressed in verse 5. But I'm grateful for those two *very little* yet powerful words, since it was for love that God predestined the believer for *"adoption to sonship"* through Christ. I also want to point out that *"sonship"* is the best way to communicate what we receive through Christ. In ancient Jewish culture, the son—*the eldest son, in fact*—was the one who inherited his father's estate. Therefore, Paul was reminding us that we gain the Father's inheritance like a *"son"*—*being co-heirs with Christ, the eldest Son.* Paul added joy upon joy by reminding us that this adoption and inheritance is according to the Lord's will through His great pleasure. I see this as circling back to God's love as the catalyst for our adoption and election.

In verse 6, Paul praised God for His *"glorious grace."* Grace is *glorious* because it is something we do not deserve, nor can derive through our own human efforts. This grace is freely given through the *"One"* God loves. Though the NIV uses the term *"One"* here, some translations use the term *"Beloved."* However, both are direct references to Christ, who is the Father's Beloved Son.

Thought to take:

I often take for granted the spiritual blessings I possess because of Christ. Sadly, I prefer earthly blessings most days. I almost always want my circumstances to be pleasant and for things to go my way. But when this is my focus, I easily *lose sight of the Lord* whenever troubles come my way. So instead I want to focus on Christ and how He has provided me with *"every"* spiritual blessing, especially when things seem to be going wrong in my life.

T2t: Count my many spiritual blessings

Help: Pray for God's help to apply your T2t both now and all day long.

Father, I never have to lapse into discouragement and despair when I can stop to realize how many spiritual blessings You shower on me from heaven. I truly am blessed! This blessing began long before You set about to form the world, when the spiritually lost were already on Your mind. Your love reached out into the future to pick me—the one who only deserved rejection and damnation. Yet You chose me because of Christ's love and sacrifice. This means I never need to worry whether I am blameless enough for You. And Your grace is not based on how impressive or successful I am either. Instead, it is based on Christ's holiness, sinless sacrifice, and victory on the cross. I'm also grateful that You find great pleasure in redeeming my life and birthing me into Your family. Your grace truly is glorious and will be my focus and praise all day long! In Jesus' name, amen.

Yield: Surrender yourself to God and His truths—reflecting on and applying your T2t all day long.

3 - A GRACE THAT KEEPS ON GIVING

Week 1, Day 3—Ephesians 1:7-10

Welcome the Lord: Ask Him to reveal His truth to you as you study.

Observe what the Scripture says:

7 - *In him we have redemption through his blood, the forgiveness of sins, in accordance with the riches of God's grace*

8 - *that he lavished on us. With all wisdom and understanding,*

9 - *he made known to us the mystery of his will according to his good pleasure, which he purposed in Christ,*

10 - *to be put into effect when the times reach their fulfillment—to bring unity to all things in heaven and on earth under Christ.*

Recognize what is noteworthy and true:

The Apostle Paul continued here to unpack the many ways that Christ is our Savior. In verse 7, Paul began by confirming that believers gain redemption through Christ's blood, which means that every sin the believer commits is forgiven by God because of the price paid by Christ. The Greek word here for *"redemption"* is *"lootruo"* and was used when speaking of paying a slave's ransom, which allowed the slave to go free. Christ had to die on the cross—*shedding His divine, sinless blood*—so that anyone who would place their faith in Him would be liberated from slavery to sin and death. The price of the ransom was so steep that only the *"riches of God's grace"* could cover the cost.

In verse 8, the NIV uses the word *"lavished" (which I really like)*, when many other translations use the term *"abound."* Both are similar to the literal Greek meaning, which indicates abounding in the most extreme sense. Or another way to think of it is to abundantly give over and over to someone. This makes it clear that God does not hold back any good thing—*especially grace*—from our lives. Paul went on to link grace with *wisdom and understanding.* Our grace comes from knowing God's *"wisdom"* revealed in the truth of the gospel. But *"understanding"* here implies that we not only trust in the truth of the gospel, but we also *apply and live out the grace and truth of the gospel.*

In verse 9, it seems as if Paul was clarifying what this wisdom and understanding stems from—*it is rooted in the mystery of God's will.* Paul reiterated that God's will was done according to what brought and brings God good pleasure. And God's good pleasure is always to redeem the lost. Therefore, the mystery of God's will and purpose are accomplished *in Christ.* As a Christ-follower, I know that Christ represents and fulfills my redemption (v. 7) and liberation from sin through His sacrifice on the cross.

However in verse 10 there is more that God accomplishes in His will and purpose through Christ. Apparently, there is a timeline yet to be reached or fulfilled. God will, one day, bring unity to all things in heaven and earth under Christ. This will be the day that Christ comes again, gathering His church *"in unity"* in the kingdom of heaven. It is then that the divisions we feel and even cling to now will be resolved. Though every believer is one with Christ now, we will also be one *with every other believer* one day. No barrier will exist between us, and complete unity will reign on that day.

Thought to take:
God's grace begins in my life at the point of my salvation and faith in Christ. However, it also continues to abound lavishly as I learn more about God's wisdom and apply His truth in my life.

So today, I will fill my heart and mind with God's good news through the study of His word *(check!)*, and then seek to apply His grace and truth in every act and encounter in my life *(to be checked at day's end!)*.

T2t: Apply the wisdom of God's word

Help: Pray for God's help to apply your T2t both now and all day long.

Dear Lord, Your plan of redemption is mind-boggling. It truly is a mystery! Yet I feel as if You have given me a peek here into Your will and plan through Christ. Your plan has been revealed through Christ's sacrifice for more than two thousand years, and yet many miss it, misunderstand it or reject it. I know that it is only through Your lavish grace that my mind can understand it. May I take the wisdom of the gospel and live it out all throughout this day. Help me to know what that means and involves, so that I can be a light to those who are still in darkness. And whenever I feel discouraged by the divisions and problems in my life today, I will meditate on and thank You for the blessed hope found in Christ. In Jesus' name I pray, amen.

Yield: Surrender yourself to God and His truths—reflecting on and applying your T2t all day long.

4 - SEALED WITH A CROSS

Week 1, Day 4—Ephesians 1:11-14

Welcome the Lord: Ask Him to reveal His truth to you as you study.

Observe what the Scripture says:

11 - *In him we were also chosen, having been predestined according to the plan of him who works out everything in conformity with the purpose of his will,*

12 - *in order that we, who were the first to put our hope in Christ, might be for the praise of his glory.*

13 - *And you also were included in Christ when you heard the message of truth, the gospel of your salvation. When you believed, you were marked in him with a seal, the promised Holy Spirit,*

14 - *who is a deposit guaranteeing our inheritance until the redemption of those who are God's possession—to the praise of his glory.*

Recognize what is noteworthy and true:

Like verse 7 earlier, here in verse 11, Paul reminded believers of what they gain and possess *"in Him"*—meaning Christ. I note that other translations leave out the term *"chosen,"* and instead say we have gained an *"inheritance,"* which is actually a better translation of the Greek here. Either way, I revel in the truth that I am *"chosen by God."* However, being chosen doesn't mean God saw me in some long line of other humans throughout history and picked me to be on His *"team."* No, He predestined or decided ahead of time—*before the world was created*—to choose me because of His *plan,* and not because of what I could bring to His plan. In God's plan, He is able to work out everything in *conformity* with *His* purpose and will. This means that I don't have to worry about whether I or someone else will wreck God's plan, since His purposes will always prevail.

Given the context in verse 12, it's important to realize that Paul was speaking from his own vantage point as a Jewish man, being among the very first people *(Jews)* to put their hope in Christ. But what I find most compelling in this verse is how Paul worded this truth. It is through the believer's hope and faith in Christ that we are able to give Him praise and glory. Everything I do as a Christ-follower should keep this aim in mind. *How can I give Christ the most praise and glory?*

In verse 13, Paul referred to the Gentiles when he said, *"you were also included,"* since Gentiles were quickly extended God's invitation soon after Christ completed His mission on the cross. The Ephesian readers here were made up of both Jew and Gentile converts to Christianity. These people heard the *"message of truth" that is the "gospel,"* which then led them to place their faith in Christ for salvation. Then they—*like every believer*—received the *"mark"* of a *"seal."* This seal promises that the Christ-follower irrefutably receives, is indwelt by and belongs to the Holy Spirit.

Verse 14, establishes the fact that the Holy Spirit also provides an irrevocable *deposit*, since this seal *"guarantees"* our inheritance in Christ. This means our redemption is not fully complete until we stand before God's throne, where we will receive our inheritance and offer our praises to Jesus. One final detail here is that every Christ-follower is God's possession. This is not to objectify anyone, but to remind us of how unified we are with Him.

Thought to take:
Sometimes I envision God watching my life unfold in my earliest days. He saw me in my crib. He saw me on my first day of school. He saw me on my wedding day. None of those days were

a surprise to Him. He is intimately acquainted with my heart, mind and life more than I could ever hope to be. *So how can I possibly resist His purpose and will?* What seems like unfair circumstances or wrong turns in my life are simply opportunities for me to trust Him more, thus bringing Him greater praise and glory by my tenacious trust in Him.

T2t: Trust God tenaciously

Help: Pray for God's help to apply your T2t both now and all day long.

Father, I want to meditate this day on how You chose and predestined me before time began. You had a plan mapped out for me long before I took my first breath. My life is not haphazard nor filled with coincidences, but rather with God-given opportunities to follow You. May that be the way I look at each situation today. Give me the ability to choose thoughts and actions that bring You glory and praise, so that others will see the *"seal"* that signifies I am Yours. Thank You for the deposit and inheritance You promise me. And empower me with Your Spirit today so that I become a better and brighter reflection of You to all I encounter and meet. In Jesus' name, amen.

Yield: Surrender yourself to God and His truths—reflecting on and applying your T2t all day long.

5 - KEY PURPOSES
OF PRAYER

Week 1, Day 5—Ephesians 1:15-17

Welcome the Lord: Ask Him to reveal His truth to you as you study.

Observe what the Scripture says:

15 - *For this reason, ever since I heard about your faith in the Lord Jesus and your love for all God's people,*

16 - *I have not stopped giving thanks for you, remembering you in my prayers.*

17 - *I keep asking that the God of our Lord Jesus Christ, the glorious Father, may give you the Spirit of wisdom and revelation, so that you may know him better.*

Recognize what is noteworthy and true:

Since Paul began verse 15 with the statement, *"For this reason,"* I'm prompted to reflect back on yesterday's reading to see and remember exactly what *reason* he pointed out. Paul had just declared that every Christ-follower was chosen before the world began, is sealed with the Holy Spirit, and is guaranteed an inheritance and place in God's family (vv. 11-14). But here, he summarized this reason by saying it was because of their *"faith in the Lord."* However, he added another thought regarding what he had heard about these people—*they loved all of God's people.* This love for other believers was an outward sign or *"mark"* of the seal of the Spirit on their lives, and is one that should be reflected in our lives as well (vv. 13-14).

Paul was such a grateful, encouraging and affirming apostle and man. In all of his letters he was sure to point out what the believers in all the churches were doing right, even when he wrote to correct them on certain issues. Here, in verse 16, is no exception. I also realize that Paul stopped to affirm these believers, even as he was sitting in a cold, dark prison cell. He must have recognized the important role of *continually* lifting them up in prayer—knowing what a difference their prayers meant for his own morale and hope in the worst of circumstances.

In verse 17, I notice that Paul gave a hint as to *how often* he prayed for these people. He *kept on* praying for them. But what's more intriguing to me is *who* he directed his request to—"*the God of our Lord Jesus Christ, the glorious Father.*" He wanted the Father—"*glorious Father*"—to hear his prayer through Christ. By this encapsulated statement, I see Christ's role emerging as the mediator between "*God and man*" (1 Tim. 2:5). I also see from this verse how Christ both gives and receives glory to and from the Father as the Son of God.

Paul requested that these believers would receive the "*Spirit of wisdom and revelation.*" Paul then gave the reason why believers need God's wisdom and revelation—*to know God better.* I seek to make the knowledge of God, gained from His word and truth, my foundation for life—*allowing every other fruit of the Spirit and reflection of Christ to flow in or shine from His truth.* These are what give Christ as well as the Father glory, but can only be ignited through our knowledge of God. I don't think Paul was talking about gaining knowledge for knowledge's sake, but rather letting the Spirit transform our minds and lives one faith-filled thought and action at a time.

Thought to take:

One major takeaway from this passage is how Paul prayed for other believers, no matter what he was going through personally. And he was so specific about what he wanted God to do in their lives—going on to ask, *not for their circumstances to remain safe or free of conflict,* but instead to have hearts that come to know God more. I want to have that same kind of concern for other believers—*lifting them up daily and especially praying that they come to know the Lord better.*

T2t: Pray continually for other believers

Help: Pray for God's help to apply your T2t both now and all day long.

Father, thank You for my transformed life, as well as for the faith of my brothers and sisters in Christ. I also realize that my faith in You must be demonstrated and proven true by my love for them, as my spiritual family. I know that one important way to love other believers is to pray for them consistently and carefully, like Paul did here. So drive that purpose and priority deeper in my life each day —*deepening my love for them as a result.* I praise You for choosing me as Your child, and as Christ's bride. I know that the only way I can truly bring glory to You and Your Son is to make Your wisdom and revelation the foundation and priority of my life. So let me never neglect to pore over and apply the Scriptures—seeking daily to know and love You more and more. In Jesus' name, amen.

Yield: Surrender yourself to God and His truths—reflecting on and applying your T2t all day long.

Week One Group Discussion Questions

1:1-2—Called and Blessed
What is one of the callings God has placed on your life, and in what ways are you living it out?

1:3-6—Showered in Heavenly Blessings
What are some of the spiritual blessings God has given you?

1:7-10—A Grace that Keeps on Giving
What remains mysterious to you about God's grace and forgiveness?

1:11-14—Sealed with a Cross
What are some of the ways you desire to live that can give Christ praise and glory?

1:15-17—Key Purposes of Prayer
How does Paul's example of praying for the spiritual growth of others influence your prayer life?

6 - CLEAR VISION AND MIGHTY MUSCLES

Week 2, Day 1—*Ephesians 1:18-20*

Welcome the Lord: Ask Him to reveal His truth to you as you study.

Observe what the Scripture says:
18 - *I pray that the eyes of your heart may be enlightened in order that you may know the hope to which he has called you, the riches of his glorious inheritance in his holy people,*
19 - *and his incomparably great power for us who believe. That power is the same as the mighty strength*
20 - *he exerted when he raised Christ from the dead and seated him at his right hand in the heavenly realms,*

Recognize what is noteworthy and true:
In the previous day's reading it was obvious *who and what* Paul was praying for. But here it seems he didn't want to leave out any detail about *how* he prayed for his dear friends. In verse 18, he told them that he prayed that the *eyes of their hearts would be enlightened*. Of course, Paul was talking in figurative terms, even though he used the Greek word for physical eyes—"*opthalmos.*" His intent was to remind believers that our hearts do, indeed, have *"eyes"* or *vision* into what God wants through the Spirit. The term *"heart"* in Scripture usually indicates the core of each person. Therefore, Paul was praying that the core and foundation of their hearts *(and ours)* would be enlightened to

God's truths.

Paul enumerated two things in this prayer for enlighten-ment (v. 18). First, he prayed for each believer's heart to see the *"hope"* to which s/he is called. I must keep my eyes focused and fixed on the calling I have through Christ as my Hope of salva-tion, as well as my hope in every trial and temptation. If I stray from my calling for even one second, I will certainly be led astray.

The second desire and prayer request listed here (v. 18) is that each believer's heart would be enlightened to the *riches* of this *"glorious inheritance."* First of all, a believer's inheritance is *rich* because we are co-heirs with all that Christ inherits (Rom. 8:17). *I cannot even begin to fathom just how rich that makes you and me!* But what we dare not miss here is that Christ considers *His* inheritance to be His *"holy"* people, and not just inheriting unparalleled wealth and position in God's kingdom. His focus was and will always be on the love He has for His bride. The final detail I see is that believers are made *"holy,"* not because of our goodness, but because of *Christ's holiness*.

In verse 19, Paul continued to remind believers of all that we gain through Christ's salvation and inheritance. Not only does Christ share His rich inheritance with me as His bride, but He also gives me *(and every believer)* incomparable *"power"* through our faith in Him. This isn't just the power to get us through some *jam* in our day, but it rises to the level of *God's mighty strength!*

If that idea wasn't enough for us, in verse 20, Paul revealed exactly how and when the Father exerted this *"mighty strength."* He exerted it when He raised Christ from the dead! He also seated Jesus at His right hand in heaven, which is a place of intimate relationship, honor and authority. I need to integrate this inspiring truth— *you and I always have, at our disposal, this level of power through the Spirit's work within us!* Wow! Just wow!

Thought to take:
It seems like Paul's letter constantly hammers upon the need to

be *enlightened in our knowledge of God.* I think that's because of how easy it is for our hearts to be deceived (Jer. 17:9). In addition to that harsh reality, I know that the *"eyes of my heart"* do not always recognize all that I *should* see. This is because I often let my own perceptions and feelings cloud my perspective. So today, I will to run to the Lord and His word whenever I'm confused or weak, so that I can clearly *"see"* what is true and what is not, as well as how to respond in the fray.

T2t: See the truth with God's eyes

Help: Pray for God's help to apply your T2t both now and all day long.

Father, open my eyes to all that You want me to see and do today. Let those truths flow from my time in Your word, where You enlighten my heart—*going on to deepen my ability to navigate life like Christ.* Let Jesus and His purposes form my core identity. And use the reality that I share a magnificent inheritance with Your Son as the inspiration that lifts me above my fears and weaknesses. *For I truly am amazed at all that You lavish on me as Your child and bride!* I never need to worry about being unable to meet the challenges of my day; for You give me the same mighty strength that You exerted when You raised Christ from the dead! *How amazing is that?!* So whenever I'm weak or in need —*which is all the time*—remind me to receive Your power that defeats every foe, fear and frustration in my life. In Jesus' name, amen.

Yield: Surrender yourself to God and His truths—reflecting on and applying your T2t all day long.

7 - HIS HIGHEST FOR OUR BEST

Week 2, Day 2—Ephesians 1:21-23

Welcome the Lord: Ask Him to reveal His truth to you as you study.

Observe what the Scripture says:
21 - *far above all rule and authority, power and dominion, and every name that is invoked, not only in the present age but also in the one to come.*
22 - *And God placed all things under his feet and appointed him to be head over everything for the church,*
23 - *which is his body, the fullness of him who fills everything in every way.*

Recognize what is noteworthy and true:
Yesterday's reading left off with the image of Christ being seated at the right hand of the Father's throne in heaven. Today, in verse 21, Paul revealed more about the extent of Christ's power. His authority and power are *"far above all rule, authority, power, and dominion"* on earth, as well as in the spiritual realm —*both then, now and forever.* To spell this out even further, it means that Christ is above every *"name"* or person on earth, as well as above every force or being—*heavenly angels, including Satan and his demons*—in the spiritual realm. This verse provides not just a statement of fact, but also gives a promise that Christ's power and authority endures forever.

In verse 22, Paul made it clear that it was God, the Father, who placed all of these powers and authorities under Christ's feet. Even as Christ was submissive and humble—*emptying Himself and coming to earth as a "servant"*—His Father demonstrates these very same qualities too. God was humble and generous enough to give the Son of God all power in heaven and in earth. There's no indication of a threat or jealousy between these two, who are One along with the Holy Spirit. I also see that the Father appointed Christ as the head over everything and everyone in the *"church."* Of course, the *"church"* here was/is not a reference to some beautiful building or cathedral, but rather to the living and breathing *"body of Christ."* This is not Christ's physical body, but His spiritual body through believers united by our faith in Him.

Of course, in verse 23, Paul correlates the body of Christ back to the *"church"* (v. 22). Every Christ-follower makes up the body of Christ (1 Cor. 12:27). If I go back and list all the other blessings and gifts Christ gives based on what Paul shared so far, I realize several things about being a Christ-follower:

1) I possess *"sonship" (better than a daughter's inheritance)* through my adoption into the family of God (v. 5).

2) I've been chosen and predestined to fulfill God's good purposes (v. 11).

3) I am sealed with a deposit of the Spirit that guarantees I am truly a child of God (vv. 13-14).

4) I make up part of His body as the *"body of Christ."*

All of this certainly gives evidence of how Christ gives the believer *"fullness"* and *"fills everything in every way."* This statement reminds me of 2 Peter 1:3 that says God's divine power has given us *"everything we need to live a godly life . . ."* But it also seems that there's more being communicated here in verse 23. As Christ-followers, we can also live an abundant life (Jn. 10:10) through Christ—both now and in eternity. *What more could we ask for?*

Thought to take:
The thought that rises to the top for me today is to stand amazed at how powerful and superior Christ is to every power known to man on earth or spiritual beings in the heavenly realms. And His boundless power is available to me as His child and bride—*filling me up in every possible way!* I never want to forget that. So I will rest in His all-encompassing power to overcome every other power that comes against me in my day.

T2t: Christ's power fills up and flows in me

Help: Pray for God's help to apply your T2t both now and all day long.

Father, what a blessing it is to know how deeply You love, trust and want to honor Your Son by giving Him the full scope of power in the universe and beyond! It reminds me of just how great, *yet humble and loving, You both are!* You did this for me and for everyone who comes to faith in Christ. And You gave Your Son the power to defeat sin in my life so that I could experience the fullness of knowing and loving You. Through Christ's sacrifice and power, I lack no good thing today, tomorrow and forever. So let me remember and meditate on that beautiful reality—*letting it encourage me when I am weak, and strengthen me when I must face opposition in life.* I know, *through Christ*, I am assured the victory; and the abundant life is mine for the taking! In Jesus' name, amen.

Yield: Surrender yourself to God and His truths—reflecting on and applying your T2t all day long.

8 - NO LONGER DEAD AND DECAYING

***Week 2, Day 3**—Ephesians 2:1-3*

Welcome the Lord: Ask Him to reveal His truth to you as you study.

Observe what the Scripture says:

1 - As for you, you were dead in your transgressions and sins,
2 - in which you used to live when you followed the ways of this world and of the ruler of the kingdom of the air, the spirit who is now at work in those who are disobedient.
3 - All of us also lived among them at one time, gratifying the cravings of our flesh and following its desires and thoughts. Like the rest, we were by nature deserving of wrath.

Recognize what is noteworthy and true:

Paul's bold and blatant approach, in verse 1, feels as if he's thrown a cold glass of water in our faces! However, it is the wake up call we all need. I notice that the word *"transgressions"* is also translated in other versions as *"trespasses."* I feel like this better communicates what our sins do—*they break the boundary-lines of God's law.* And Paul certainly wanted every believer to come to terms with the fact that we were *"dead"* in our *"transgressions and sins"* before coming to Christ. Our holy God could and would not draw near to a sin-stained *"corpse,"* putrid with the stench of death! That's how disgusting our spiritual lives were to God before coming to Christ.

In verse 2, Paul wanted to remind believers just whom we were following in our former lives as unbelievers. First of all, we followed the *"ways of this world."* This means we followed the way other humans and our culture lived—*based solely in human logic and unbridled desire.* We also followed the *"ruler of the kingdom of the air, the spirit who is now at work in those who are disobedient."* This is an obvious reference to Satan. Although Christ defeated Satan through His death and resurrection, Satan's influence and limited power are still in effect until Christ returns. The enemy's impact and influence is greater on unbelievers, but obviously, demonic forces tempt *believers* every day as well. Every time I give into Satan's temptations, I become like the one Paul described as *"disobedient."* However, *with Christ in me*, I possess the power to resist and reject Satan's schemes. You and I must make the conscious choice to resist Satan, so that God can draw near to us (James 4:7).

In verse 3, Paul humbly and honestly admitted how he, as well as these believers, lived among the spiritually dead before their salvation. Of course, this is also true of *every* believer's former life before Christ. Since Paul was a legalistic Pharisee before his conversion, it's hard for me to imagine that he ever *gratified the cravings of his flesh and followed its desires and thoughts.* Yet, I'm sure he sinned by idolizing the religious laws. And, certainly, his persecution and execution of believers, before coming to Christ, were as black as any depravity can get! Therefore, his sobering statement, *"We were by nature deserving of [God's] wrath"* expresses exactly how God feels about every sin you and I commit. However, this was and is *not just a feeling* for God, but also a statement about *what we deserve* for our sins—*damnation in hell.* Thankfully, the the Father looks at every believer through the love and shed blood of Christ, who satisfied God's wrath by redeeming our souls from sin and death.

Thought to take:
What my heart is drawn to from this reading is the reality of my

life before coming to Christ. To put it bluntly—*I was spiritually dead!* This moves me to strive for a deeper understanding of how powerful and impactful the Holy Spirit's work is and has been in my life. He resurrected my soul from sin and saves me from the flames of hell—*going further to purify my life so that the Father can embrace me!* I will reflect on all that my saving relationship with Jesus means—*honoring and celebrating it all throughout my day!*

T2t: Honor and celebrate Christ's gift to me

Help: Pray for God's help to apply your T2t both now and all day long.

Father, I don't know how You could have loved me when I was dead in my sins. I was like an empty and hollow corpse without one worthwhile quality or characteristic to draw a holy and all-powerful God to me. In that former life apart from You, I only thought about myself, and what would bring me pleasure and gain. I also let the world define who I was and how I lived. Worse still, I let the whispers of Satan mold my view of You—*believing the lie that Your ways are far too stringent and fanatical to embrace.* But as soon as I came to faith in You, it was like You turned on all the lights in my heart and mind—*awakening me and saving me from the grip of death.* I still struggle to comprehend all that You are and offer me, because Your ways are so far above my own. But now I thank You for that disparity—*for Your might and superiority over all powers and persons in life.* Use that reality to strengthen my ability to take every action and thought captive to Your will and ways today. It's the least that I can do for the God who came down to earth and now lives in my heart. In Jesus' name, amen.

Yield: Surrender yourself to God and His truths—reflecting on and applying your T2t all day long.

9 - SEATED WITH JESUS IN HEAVEN

Week 2, Day 4—*Ephesians 2:4-7*

Welcome the Lord: Ask Him to reveal His truth to you as you study.

Observe what the Scripture says:
4 - *But because of his great love for us, God, who is rich in mercy,*
5 - *made us alive with Christ even when we were dead in transgressions—it is by grace you have been saved.*
6 - *And God raised us up with Christ and seated us with him in the heavenly realms in Christ Jesus,*
7 - *in order that in the coming ages he might show the incomparable riches of his grace, expressed in his kindness to us in Christ Jesus.*

Recognize what is noteworthy and true:
Today's reading prompts me to refresh my memory of yesterday's reading, since verse 4 reveals the motivation for why God could and would *turn from His wrath* due to our sin (v. 3). First, it is because of God's *love* for us; and second, it is because God is rich in *mercy*. I cannot overlook what is not listed here as His motive. It is not because you and I are lovable or good in and of ourselves. It is only because God's love and mercy are so great that He would give His only Son for us—*the broken and dead, who betrayed Him from the start.*

Verse 5 seems to reflect what Paul said in verse 1—reminding us that *"we were dead in transgressions."* But now every Christ-

33

follower *is alive* because of Christ, who saves us by *grace*. There's one important nuance to the way Paul worded this that is worthy of notice: A believer's salvation isn't something *initiated by the believer*. Instead, it is initiated by God, the Father (v. 4) who *"made us alive even when we were dead"* in our sin (v. 5). This means that God resurrects us like He resurrected Christ from the dead. God does this miracle of salvation *by His grace*. Making it clear that salvation cannot be earned and is not deserved by any human, since God's grace actually means *unmerited favor*.

Verse 6 is one of my favorite verses in the Bible, because it reveals an awesome and inspiring truth and reality for every Christ-follower. Since this verse is stated in the present tense, it tells me that it is a current reality in the spiritual realm. Therefore, as a believer, this means that I am raised up with Christ and seated with Him in the heavenly realms, even though my feet are firmly planted on the soil of earth. These are things that are beyond my comprehension as a human trapped in time. *But could it be that I am sitting right now with Christ, chatting about my life on earth?* I don't know. But I *do know* that my heart is with Christ and He is with my heart, *both here and heavenward*.

In verse 7, Paul turned our focus toward *"the coming ages"*— *meaning future generations*. God is always looking to show His *incomparable riches of grace* to a watching world every single day. This is the hallmark and constant reflection of His loving heart. God also continually expresses kindness to us. This kindness is due to the sacrifice that Christ completed and provides to all who receive His salvation. I'm grateful that the Lord is patient for thousands of years to pass in order to give one more soul the blessing of His gracious salvation.

Thought to take:

I often neglect considering what a sacrifice it was and is for the Father and Son to extend love, mercy and grace to the spiritually dead, *living in rebellion against Him*. After all, I have trouble extending grace and mercy to those who hurt me in much less damaging and hateful ways than how I've hurt and rejected Christ! But that is *not God's approach*, since He expresses and initiates grace at all times to all generations. So I will make it my aim today to extend love, mercy and grace to all in my life.

T2t: Extend love, mercy and grace to all

Help: Pray for God's help to apply your T2t both now and all day long.

Father, what a blessing it is to know that You love me in such a profoundly sacrificial way. Your overwhelming love and mercy demanded that You extend grace to me, even when I was still dead in my sins and shaking my fist in Your merciful face. *How can that be?* The only explanation is that it is through Christ and the perfect work of redemption that He completed on the cross for me. *Thank You for that wonderful gift!* And thank You for raising me from spiritual death to *new life in You* here on earth. Thank You also for raising me up to where Christ is seated in the heavenly realms. My mind cannot comprehend this truth; *but I rejoice and revel in this reality just the same!* Use it to encourage and strengthen me in my resolve to follow You, as well as giving me the ability to express Your same love, mercy and grace to all who are in my life each day. In Jesus' name, amen.

Yield: Surrender yourself to God and His truths—reflecting on and applying your T2t all day long.

10 - GOD FUELS MY GOOD

Week 2, Day 5—*Ephesians 2:8-10*

Welcome the Lord: Ask Him to reveal His truth to you as you study.

Observe what the Scripture says:
8 - *For it is by grace you have been saved, through faith—and this is not from yourselves, it is the gift of God—*
9 - *not by works, so that no one can boast.*
10 - *For we are God's handiwork, created in Christ Jesus to do good works, which God prepared in advance for us*

Recognize what is noteworthy and true:
Paul continued to unpack, in verse 8, how the grace of God saves those who believe. I find it interesting that God's grace works "*through*" our faith. I think this is like saying that faith is the vehicle of our salvation, while God's grace is like the fuel that makes the vehicle move. Without God's grace working through and in the vehicle of our faith, we would never get anywhere. This makes it absolutely clear that I cannot attain my salvation, but rather God initiates it as His "*gift*" to me.

The reasons why the Lord chose to construct salvation in this way are revealed in verse 9. First, God ensures that salvation cannot be won or earned by any good *work* or totality of works that a person has done in his/her lifetime. This is because God's salvation is a *gift* (v.8). It can only be received, rather than bought or achieved, *since Christ already paid the steep price for our precious salvation.* It is a price that I, *as a flawed and sinful human*

37

being, could never afford or attain without Christ.

The next reason revealed (v. 9) is so that *"no one can boast"* about any human accomplishment, no matter how noble or helpful. There must be total surrender and dependence on Christ at our point of salvation and onward. I also see and understand that I can never achieve anything of any good without God being the One to empower me for that task. Therefore, He must be like the fuel in the engine of my vehicle—*igniting my salvation, and then going on to fuel my efforts to do any good works*. This protects me against developing pride, since God opposes the proud (1 Peter 5:5).

However, in verse 10, I find it hard *not to feel a good sense of pride* and joy in the fact that God calls every Christ-follower His *"handiwork"* (NIV). Other translations use words like: workmanship, masterpiece, and creation to describe who and what we are *through* Christ. Most agree that this is about God declaring His ownership as the Master Creator of our new life in Christ. And as our Master Creator, He is and has been the One to do *all good works through us*. We cannot take credit for any good that we do, since it is only accomplished through God's enablement working within us.

Another fascinating fact is revealed in this verse—God *prepared*, or some translations say *"ordained,"* in advance for us to do certain good works. I take this to mean that not only did God choose every Christ-follower before the world was ever created, He also chose the good works that He would do through us in our lifetimes. This is an exciting truth, since it means that God is constantly orchestrating my next opportunity to do the good He chose for me to do before He created the world. Therefore, you and I must always anticipate His promptings and respond with obedience to them.

Thought to take:

This reading reminds me to take note of the good works God has done in my life and enables me to do every single day. I will do this, *not in a prideful way,* but in a way that opens my eyes to God's empowerment and opportunities in every situation. I will then thank Him for these divinely appointed opportunities, as well as for the power He gives me to accomplish the tasks that He prepared for me to do before time began.

T2t: Do the good God wants me to do

Help: Pray for God's help to apply your T2t both now and all day long.

Father, Your word makes it very clear that my salvation or any good that I do in this life cannot be achieved by my own efforts. You were the One to ignite my new life in Christ, and You are the Master Creator who provides the fuel to move me toward all the good works You prepared in advance for me to do. So open my eyes to the many divine appointments You place in my path; then remind me to rely on Your power alone to do each good work. As soon as I accomplish Your will, may I stop to thank You for that gift—*resisting any prideful focus.* For I want to always give You the credit and glory for any good I do in life. It is the least that I can do for the God who loves, chose and skillfully created me. In Jesus' name, amen.

Yield: Surrender yourself to God and His truths—reflecting on and applying your T2t all day long.

Week Two Group Discussion Questions

1:18-20—Clear Vision and Mighty Muscles
How is God's word providing a clearer vision for what to do in a particular situation?

1:21-23—His Highest for Our Best
How does knowing that Jesus is *"far above all rule, authority, power and dominion"* encourage you in the challenging situations you are facing in life?

2:1-3—No Longer Dead and Decaying
What remains mysterious to you about God's grace and forgiveness?

2:4-7—Seated with Jesus in Heaven
What are some of the actions and attitudes you want to change or begin to do, so that your life gives Christ greater praise and glory?

2:8-10—God Fuels My Good
How does Paul's example of praying for the spiritual growth of others inspire you? What do you think can happen if you don't follow his example?

11 - HOW FAR AWAY
YOU WERE

Week 3, Day 1—Ephesians 2:11-13

Welcome the Lord: Ask Him to reveal His truth to you as you study.

Observe what the Scripture says:
11 - *Therefore, remember that formerly you who are Gentiles by birth and called "uncircumcised" by those who call themselves "the circumcision" (which is done in the body by human hands)—*
12 - *remember that at that time you were separate from Christ, excluded from citizenship in Israel and foreigners to the covenant of the promise, without hope and without God in the world.*

Recognize what is noteworthy and true:
It's important to remember that Paul's letter was written to the church in Ephesus that was made up of both Jewish and Gentile believers. So here in verse 11, he turned his focus from the entire body of believers (in the previous verses), to singling out the Gentiles among them—*asking them to remember who they were formerly before Christ.* Obviously, they were Gentiles by *physical birth*, which meant they were also called *"uncircumcised"* by the Jews because most, *if not all of the men,* were uncircumcised. Paul stated it this way because the Jews considered themselves to be from an elite and superior group known as *"the circumcision."* However, Paul was not highlighting this for the sake of putting the Gentiles in their place. Instead, he wanted to remind *all* the believers that circumcision does not save, nor

signify salvation. It was a *"human"* act of obedience to the Law or Old Covenant, which Christ replaced with the New Covenant through His death on the cross.

In verse 12, Paul reminded the Gentiles of their humble beginnings as unbelievers. Before they came to faith, they were *"separate from Christ, excluded from citizenship in Israel and foreigners to the covenant of the promise."* I want to skip over the fact that they were separate from Christ—*returning to it in a minute*—to note what being excluded from *"citizenship in Israel"* meant. Paul was pointing out that the Gentiles were not originally included as God's chosen people or partakers of the promise of Christ, like the Jews were at one time. But all of that changed when Christ's salvation was extended to Gentiles, as well as the Jews (Romans 9:6-13). Now every believer in Christ is considered to be one of God's *"chosen people."* And I believe that also means Gentile believers were *chosen before the world was ever formed*, as well as their Jewish brothers and sisters in the faith (Eph. 1:11).

In verse 12, the statement, *"foreigners to the covenant of the promise,"* refers to the promise of the Messiah that the New Covenant *now* offers to *every* believer. However, before this was extended to Gentiles, they were foreigners to that important promise of salvation found in Christ alone!

Now, back to the most compelling and disturbing part here (v. 12)—the Gentiles were separated from Christ before coming to Him in faith. As a believer, this idea stirs up tremendous sadness within me, but also gladness that I'm united with Jesus *now* through my faith in Him. I'm sure it had the same bittersweet impact on these believing Gentiles. Going further in verse 12, Paul reminded them that they were also *without hope* in the world, because they were *without God*. The world is a harsh and *hopeless* place without God giving us hope through His salvation.

Thought to take:

I'm so glad that God didn't stop at extending the New Covenant and promise of hope only to Jewish people, but instead offers this promise and gift of salvation to me and every other Gentile *(non-Jew)* as well. With Christ as my Savior and Promise-keeper, it means I never walk alone, am separated from the Lord, nor remain a foreigner to His grace and hope. I will bask in the truth that He is always with me—*lovingly guiding and empowering me with His Spirit.*

T2t: God and His hope are always with me

Help: Pray for God's help to apply your T2t both now and all day long.

Father, I never want to forget how far You have brought me from when I was lost and without Your saving grace. Before You drew me near, I was trying to win Your acceptance by human means. But that can never be enough to satisfy a holy and perfect God. I needed to be so much more than that for You to accept and draw near to me. So You sent Your Son to be the *"More"* that the lost world needed—*that I desperately needed!* Thank You for giving me the privilege of being among Your chosen people—redeemed by Your Son's blood. Your love compelled You to draw me near, to save my soul through Your Son's death on the cross, and to adopt me into Your family because of my faith in Christ. So I will bask in the reality that You are always with me today —*providing the freedom and forgiveness that I constantly need.* In Jesus' name, amen.

Yield: Surrender yourself to God and His truths—reflecting on and applying your T2t all day long.

12 - PEACE FLOWING IN AND OUT

Week 3, Day 2—Ephesians 2:13-14

Welcome the Lord: Ask Him to reveal His truth to you as you study.

Observe what the Scripture says:
13 - *But now in Christ Jesus you who once were far away have been brought near by the blood of Christ.*
14 - *For he himself is our peace, who made the two groups one and has destroyed the barrier, the dividing wall of hostility,*

Recognize what is noteworthy and true:
The truth and reality of verse 13 swells my heart with joy at the thought! Every Christ-follower—*Gentile or Jew*—that was far away from Jesus has now been *"brought near by the blood of Christ."* I no longer go through this life alone. The Spirit is my constant Companion, Caretaker and Counselor. I also love the idea that is implied in this verse. It sounds as if Christ could not stand the distance and divide that separated the lost from Him. He was willing to go to the extreme of shedding His precious blood and dying on the cross—*being branded as a criminal and heretic, as well*—all because He wanted to bring His lost ones near to His sword-pierced side (Luke 15:4).

It's also important to understand the significance and need for the *shedding of blood.* The Old Covenant involved sacrificing and slaying a blemish-free animal on the altar, which represented the sacrifice of Christ—*as the "Lamb of God*—to cover the sins committed by the sinner. This, however, was a temporary solution. With Christ's perfect and completed sacrifice on the cross, He was able to replace forever that inferior practice—going further to fulfill the promise of salvation for all who place their faith in Him.

I feel like verse 14 would be hard to fully understand without first understanding and referring to the context of this entire passage. We must remember that Paul had been talking (vv. 11-13) about the division between the Jews and Gentiles up to this point and verse. So he would continue here in verse 14 to unpack the significance of Christ's impact upon *both* of these groups of people—*saying Christ destroyed the barrier between them and brought peace.* This holds *two* meanings. The first one is that God brought peace between Jews and Gentiles. Sadly, there's still so much hatred and hostility between differing Christian groups, and yet here we are told that Christ's death put an end to that hostility. This reminds me that when I do not embrace another Christ-follower—*especially anyone who differs on the non-essentials of my faith*—I am ignoring the huge sacrifice Christ paid to bring us together into His beloved family. I want to keep my heart and mind focused on the peace Christ has brought, not just to my life, but also to my family of faith.

However, the most important truth of verse 14 is that this "*hostility*" also represented what once existed between the *lost and God (We will see in more detail in tomorrow's reading what this hostility represented).* Thankfully, Christ's death and resurrection destroyed the barrier and hostility between God and us. To put this in a more personal light, as an unbeliever, I was God's enemy. But as a believer, I have been bought by Christ's blood, brought near by His love, and am now adopted into His divine family. *Can't get any better than that!*

Thought to take:
I am moved by the fact that Christ destroyed the barrier and re-

moved the hostility that once existed between God and myself, as well as between other believers and myself. So as a Christ-follower, I need to pursue His peace in every difficulty I face in my life—remembering He has brought me near to His side. I know this realization will stir up the peace my anxious heart feels in every strife-filled moment. But I also want to pursue His peace in my relationship with other believers. When others look at me today, I want them to see Christ's peace flowing in and through me to them!

T2t: Let Christ's peace flow in and through me

Help: Pray for God's help to apply your T2t both now and all day long.

Father, You are such a peace-loving and peacemaking God! You could not stand the hostility and barrier that stood between Yourself and the lost. And I am so grateful that You did not leave the lost world locked out of Your grace and forgiveness. For Your love compelled You to send Your Son to die so that salvation and freedom could be ours. For I know that my life and actions before coming to Your grace made me Your enemy —*causing You great pain.* But thankfully Christ was willing to endure the full extent of pain possible, so that I would be brought near to His pierced side through His salvation and grace. May I never go a minute in this day without remembering that cost and the huge blessing that it means for me! Let the peace that Christ brings permeate every anxious moment in my day, as well as empowering me to be a peacemaker in all of my relationships, but especially with other believers. In Jesus' name, amen.

Yield: Surrender yourself to God and His truths—reflecting on and applying your T2t all day long.

13 - OUR HOSTILITY, HIS PEACE

Week 3, Day 3—*Ephesians 2:15-16*

Welcome the Lord: Ask Him to reveal His truth to you as you study.

Observe what the Scripture says:
15 - *by setting aside in his flesh the law and its commands and regulations. His purpose was to create in himself one new humanity out of the two, thus making peace,*
16 - *and in one body to reconcile both of them to God through the cross, by which he put to death their hostility.*

Recognize what is noteworthy and true:
In verse 15, Paul identified that this barrier represented not just the barrier of our sin, but also the *"law and its commands and regulations" (represented by the Old Covenant).* This barrier also went on to separate us from each other and the Lord. It did this by dividing Jew and Gentile in their belief systems, as well as separating every sinner from a holy God. But Christ set this barrier aside when He came in human form *(in the flesh)* to earth. This reminds me of how important it is to guard against looking to any religious act to save me/us. Since Christ set this barrier of religious activity aside and triumphs over it with His death and resurrection, *we need no other effort or power than Christ!*
Further down in verse 15, I see that Jesus' purpose was to create in Himself *"one new humanity"* (NIV), which I believe is

49

better translated, *"made two into one."* This *"one"* is the unified church that has been reconciled (v. 16) or melded from what were originally two separate groups. Now, every believer—*Jew and Gentile*—is one in Christ, serving as His body and as the church. By destroying the barrier and removing the hostility, Christ establishes *"peace"* among the body of believers.

In verse 16, Paul revealed that this *"one body"* is *"reconciled"* to God. Being reconciled means we can coexist in harmony and peace with the other members of Christ's body, as well as with our God. The offenses and sins we've committed against each other and God are paid for and covered by Christ's sacrifice. The truth is, the blending and unifying of these two groups into Christ's body results in something higher and greater than we could ever be or do on our own. Through Christ's redemption, every believer is able to find peace with each other and experience peace in our hearts, *because we are now at peace with God.* However, this oneness in Christ, as the church, is only partially fulfilled for us today. In Ephesians 1:10, Paul revealed that when the fullness of time comes, Christ will *"bring unity to all things."* This is a reference to Christ bringing total unity and oneness to the church one day—in the *"fullness of time."* I can certainly see that there is a degree of distance and discord present among Christ's body today, though we have the power to be unified in Christ.

Near the end of this verse, Paul referenced once again Christ putting to death *their hostility.* I take this to mean that Christ put to death all that creates animosity and separation between differing groups of believers, since every Christ-follower has been made one with Him. Any discontentment, discouragement or disappointment *"can"* be replaced with His peace, *if and when* we turn to Him and let Him reign in our hearts, circumstances and relationships.

Thought to take:
This reading reminds me to set aside any pettiness or hostility I

feel against other believers, since they too are a part of Christ's body and one with me as a believer. I will remember that Christ paid the highest and most painful of prices to bring me—*to bring us*—close and into His family, so that we can experience His peace in all sorts of ways and relationships. My aim today will be to pursue Christ and His peace in my heart, my relationships, but also in particular in my relationships *with other believers.* I will recognize that sometimes peace with other believers may not come because this promise is only partially fulfilled at this present time. So until the fullness of time comes, I will do my part to pursue peace in all of my relationships and leave the rest up to Jesus.

T2t: Pursue Christ's peace

Help: Pray for God's help to apply your T2t both now and all day long.

Father, so many times I go looking for peace in this life, when Your Son became Peace for me. *I want to bask in that truth!* I also thank Jesus for being willing to empty Himself and take on flesh and bone—*walking among us who rejected, reviled and ultimately crucified Him*—so that every believer can be unified with Him. How wonderful it is that He let no barrier stand in His way of that monumental task! Let Christ's victory draw me together with my Christian brothers and sisters in a tight bond. Above all, I praise You that Jesus, as my Prince of Peace, enables me to experience peace inwardly, no matter how long conflict rages outwardly. In Jesus' name, amen.

Yield: Surrender yourself to God and His truths—reflecting on and applying your T2t all day long.

14 - CHRIST OPENED THE DOOR

Week 3, Day 4—Ephesians 2:17-19

Welcome the Lord: Ask Him to reveal His truth to you as you study.

Observe what the Scripture says:

17 - *He came and preached peace to you who were far away and peace to those who were near.*

18 - *For through him we both have access to the Father by one Spirit.*

19 - *Consequently, you are no longer foreigners and strangers, but fellow citizens with God's people and also members of his household,*

Recognize what is noteworthy and true:

In yesterday's reading Paul was highlighting the work Christ accomplished through His death on the cross. But today's focus here, in verse 17, seems to take a look back on the events in Christ's life *before* His crucifixion. In keeping with the context that Paul introduced in this chapter, it is evident that he was still speaking directly to the Gentile and Jewish believers in Ephesus, even though his message was and is for *every* generation since.

In verse 17, Paul spoke directly to the Gentile believers— *saying that Christ had come and preached to them ("those") who were far away from the Lord.* The Gentiles had no concept of the true and living God found in Christ before coming to faith in Him. They were mostly, *if not all*, pagan worshippers, who had

completely centered their lives around their idolatrous practices and hedonistic desires before their conversion. Based on
the gospel accounts, it's clear how often the Gentiles or foreigners *(those who were far away)* were among the crowds hearing
Jesus' preaching.

Paul also pointed out that Christ preached *"peace to those
who were near"*—referring to the Jews who might have been in
those crowds listening to Jesus as well.Christ had preached the
"gospel of peace" (Eph. 6:15) to them, because the gospel message invites all to experience the *peace* of God through Christ. I
would say the reason the Jews were considered *"near"* was because they had been worshipping the one, true God in their Jewish practices, even before Christ secured salvation on the cross.
After trusting in Christ, they went from being *near* Him to being
indwelt by Him through the Holy Spirit.

In verse 18, Paul recapped what he had said in verses 14-16
—reminding the Ephesians *and us* that both the Jew and Gentile
share access to the Father by the one Spirit of Christ, who in-
dwells every believer. Christ has opened wide the door for us.
Now, if believers are fully surrendered and open to the Spirit's
voice and leading, we will hear and do the same things; for the
Spirit of God is one of unity and singular purpose. Though believers may have differences on the nonessentials of our faith,
we can experience unity and oneness on the essentials of our
faith through the Spirit.

In verse 19, Paul turned his focus directly again to the Gentile believers among the recipients of this letter when he said
they were *"no longer foreigners and strangers, but fellow citizens
with God's people."* Most likely, the Gentile Ephesian believers
felt rejection from the Jewish believers *("God's people")* among
them, who doubted their acceptance by Christ. If and when this
was the case, Paul made it clear how accepted and embraced
they *(and we)* are in the *"household"* of God—*regardless of their/
our race or background.* It is through our shared faith in Christ
that we are brought near and *brought in.*

Thought to take:
I am so grateful for the direct access that Christ made possible for each believer—opening the door to where the Father is and welcoming us in. This reminds me that I have the attention of the Spirit of God at any given moment, and He watches over me even when I am not aware of Him or His abiding presence. That's something no other religious *"god"* or power offers or *desires* to offer. So today I will remember that I have access to my heavenly Father, and will walk through that open door—*making myself at home in His presence.*

T2t: Access my Father all day long

Help: Pray for God's help to apply your T2t both now and all day long.

Father, I am amazed by all that You give me as Your child. You didn't just save me from the flames of hell, but were compelled to lavish me—*and every child of Yours—with infinite spiritual blessings.* The most tender of these blessings is that I have access through Jesus to You! What a joy it is to know that You want to draw me near and wrap Your arms around me every moment of my life. And I want to position myself to hear the whispers of Your love for me all throughout this day. I truly do hear those loving whispers leaping off the pages of my Bible and bowling me over with Your affection for me. *This means the world to me!* So I thank You for adopting and welcoming me into Your family as well. Keep that reality in the forefront of my mind as I interact with and pray throughout my day for my brothers and sisters in Christ. I will make it my aim to drop any defenses I have against those who've hurt me—*knowing the price You paid to make us one.* In Jesus' name, amen.

Yield: Surrender yourself to God and His truths—reflecting on and applying your T2t all day long.

15 - BUILD MY LIFE
ON CHRIST

Week 3, Day 5—Ephesians 2:20-22

Welcome the Lord: Ask Him to reveal His truth to you as you study.

Observe what the Scripture says:
20 - *built on the foundation of the apostles and prophets, with Christ Jesus himself as the chief cornerstone.*
21 - *In him the whole building is joined together and rises to become a holy temple in the Lord.*
22 - *And in him you too are being built together to become a dwelling in which God lives by his Spirit.*

Recognize what is noteworthy and true:
Today's reading requires a quick look back at verses 17-19 to understand Paul's continued thought here in verse 20, where Paul revealed the first aspect of the foundation. The *"household"* or family of God is built upon the foundation of *"apostles and prophets."* This is because they faithfully brought and revealed God's message to the people. This reminds me that it is imperative, as a member of the body of Christ and His household, to build my faith upon the teachings and prophecies now recorded in God's word. I also see that, as the foundation of our faith, the apostles and prophets carry some of the weight of the *"church"* or body of believers in a sense. But they were/are only able to do this as they stand atop Christ as their and our immutable and ir-

replaceable *"chief cornerstone."*

In verse 21, I note that Paul explained what the purpose was and is for the *chief cornerstone*. Every building has a chief cornerstone that is placed at the tip of the angle of the building—holding the entire structure in place. It is considered to be the most important stone in every structure—*even more important than the foundation*. That fits *(pardon the pun)* and further illustrates what Paul was saying here about the whole building being *joined together*. Furthermore, not only is the household of God joined together through Christ, Paul reminded us that believers rise to become a *"holy temple in the Lord."* What a stunning truth and comforting image this is for every believer!

In verse 22, Paul went on to clearly delineate who, *not what*, exactly makes up this holy temple. Christ-followers are all *"being built together to become a dwelling in which God lives by his spirit."* Many attribute the building in which people worship God as *"the church"* or as *"the temple."* But truly, *and more importantly*, every Christ-follower makes up the holy temple of God. I believe this is because the Holy Spirit now takes up residence within each believer. Therefore, there is no longer a need for the *"holy of holies"* to be hidden away behind a curtain and constructed within the walls of a temple. As Christ-followers, we are not made of brick and mortar, but flesh and bone infused with the Spirit of God—becoming and existing as His holy dwelling place. Our hearts are His *"holy of holies."*

I also note that Paul stated the idea of *"being built"* as a continuous action. This reminds me that God desires for me to share my faith, doing my part to bring others into the household of God that is *continually being built* with new believers into His dwelling place.

Thought to take:
The main idea that I notice from this passage is that my faith must be built upon the truths and prophecies that have been recorded and revealed in the Scriptures—all secured and fulfilled

by Christ. I dare not take this for granted, nor leave a single brick out of that foundation—*most importantly, building my faith upon Christ.* So I will make efforts today to build my life, attitudes and actions upon God's truth and Christ's power in me. This should also be reflected in how I am a continual witness for Him.

T2t: Build my life on God and His word

Help: Pray for God's help to apply your T2t both now and all day long.

Father, help me to apply these truths that Your word reveals to me today. Give me greater insight and inspiration into what it means to build my life on the truth of Your word, and ultimately on Christ as my chief cornerstone. Give me opportunities to integrate and apply this amazing truth to every situation and conflict I encounter today—*deepening my faith and solidifying Your foundation in my life.* I also pray that I would recognize the wonder and joy of being built into Your holy temple with my brothers and sisters in Christ. Teach me to yield and surrender my heart to the greater unity and together-ness You continually weave into the household of faith. I must do my part not only to let go of any bitterness toward other believers, but also to share my faith with those You desire to build into Your holy temple. So strengthen and encourage me for each of these important tasks today. In Jesus' name, amen.

Yield: Surrender yourself to God and His truths—reflecting on and applying your T2t all day long.

Week Three Group Discussion Questions

2:11-13—How Far Away You Were
How can you better integrate the truth that Christ has brought you near?

2:13-14—Peace Flowing In and Out
What would help you to rely more on Christ to bring peace into your relationships, attitudes and circumstances?

2:15-16—Our Hostility, His Peace
In what ways are you relying on your own efforts to achieve peace in your relationships? In what ways have you been able to rely on the peace Christ has already brought to your relationships?

2:17-19—Christ Opened the Door
How does being included in the household of faith change the way you view other believers? How can it change the way you interact with them moving forward?

2:20-22—Build My Life on Christ
How are you doing on relying and applying God's truth each day? How are you doing on sharing your faith with others—*building up the household of faith?* What can you do to improve on both of these fronts?

16 - GOD LETS US IN
ON HIS SECRET

Week 4, Day 1—Ephesians 3:1-3

Welcome the Lord: Ask Him to reveal His truth to you as you study.

Observe what the Scripture says:

1 - For this reason I, Paul, the prisoner of Christ Jesus for the sake of you Gentiles—

2 - Surely you have heard about the administration of God's grace that was given to me for you,

3 - that is, the mystery made known to me by revelation, as I have already written briefly.

Recognize what is noteworthy and true:

Chapter three opens here, in verse 1, with Paul reminding the Ephesian believers that he is *(was)* a prisoner. In two ways this was very true, but not in the way these people might have immediately expected. After all, Paul was imprisoned under house arrest while writing this particular letter. Even though he could move about the house during the day—*though never leaving its premises*—during the night hours, he was chained to a Roman guard. Still, Paul did not focus on this harsh reality, but rather focused on the beautiful and blessed reality that he was a *prisoner of Christ*. He did not let the Romans or any other man or manmade belief system imprison his heart and mind. Paul demonstrated the kind of higher focus and joyful devotion that we all should strive for in every ongoing trial and unfair loss in life.

Paul gave a curious reason for why he was a prisoner of Christ—*it was for the sake of the Gentiles.* This could be taken as an indictment of the Gentiles—blaming them for his *"chains."* However, Paul was not condemning, nor criticizing this people group. Paul was completely willing to suffer for the Lord so that the gospel would be preached to all—*including to the Gentiles, who were once considered inferior and loathsome to the Jews.* He suffered for the sake of others, just like Christ suffered for us.

In verse 2, the first layer to Paul's focus was on how these Gentile believers had heard about the *"administration of God's grace"* given to him. After all, his many missionary efforts to the Gentiles were widely known by them at this point. It's also important to note that the *"administration of God's grace"* is better-translated *"stewardship of God's grace."* This means that Paul was entrusted with the call to implement God's strategy for reaching the Gentiles with *"God's grace" (meaning the gospel).* This is in contrast to the Apostle Peter's call to *reach the Jews* with the gospel (Gal. 2:8). Both callings were needed and of equal value to God. Therefore, we should value each other's different callings as well.

Paul called this strategy to reach the Gentiles with the gospel a *"mystery"* in verse 3. Though the English meaning of the word *"mystery"* evokes the sense that we can never know the answers to something dark and hidden, the Greek meaning of this word involves a secret that is *no longer guarded or hidden.* God took what was a secret and revealed it *by way of a miraculous revelation* to Paul. In Galatians 1:15-16 and 2:2, Paul spoke about how that revelation occurred near the start of his faith walk with the Lord. Here in chapter 3:3, Paul also referred back to when he had briefly mentioned this amazing *mystery* in Ephesians 1:10.

Thought to take:

I'm moved by Paul's unselfish devotion and submission to Christ—*being willing to suffer in such a monumental way for the spreading of the gospel.* So I *too* will embrace being a prisoner of Christ. My life is not my own, and I really do not have the right to make choices based upon my own freewill—*being devoted solely to Christ's will instead.* Keeping with this metaphor, it's as if I should never leave the household of God, nor step away from His constant guard over my heart and life. So today I will strive to set aside *my* desires whenever they conflict with Christ's.

T2t: Chain my heart and actions to Jesus

Help: Pray for God's help to apply your T2t both now and all day long.

Father, not in a million years would I ever choose on my own to become a prisoner. Yet with Your grace and love filling every room in the household of faith, I have been compelled to run through that door—*letting You lock it tightly behind me.* So I pray that You would keep the desire to be Your servant and prisoner ablaze in my heart every day of my life! Fuel my devotion to You and Your purposes, even when pain threatens to consume me and losses sear my soul. For it is the least I can do—*submitting and yielding to You and Your precious will!* I also want to thank You for extending Your grace not just to Jews, but to Gentiles as well. For without that open door in Your redemptive plan, I would never have known the joy of being Your child and included in the household of faith. So I will spend my days praising You for that gift of grace lavished on me, as well as on all who call upon You for salvation. In Jesus' name, amen.

Yield: Surrender yourself to God and His truths—reflecting on and applying your T2t all day long.

17 - REST IN AND WRESTLE WITH GOD

Week 4, Day 2—*Ephesians 3:4-6*

Welcome the Lord: Ask Him to reveal His truth to you as you study.

Observe what the Scripture says:
4 - *In reading this, then, you will be able to understand my insight into the mystery of Christ,*
5 - *which was not made known to people in other generations as it has now been revealed by the Spirit of God's holy apostles and prophets.*
6 - *This mystery is that through the gospel the Gentiles are heirs together with Israel, members together of one body, and sharers together in the promise in Christ Jesus.*

Recognize what is noteworthy and true:
It is encouraging here, in verse 4, to see how Paul trusted that these believers were reading his letter and considering his words on this matter. I also note that he linked this action to their *understanding* of the mystery of Christ. There are so many mysteries of God contained in the Bible, but they will remain forever overlooked, unknown and confusing to those who do not take the time to read and discover them. This particular mystery is about how God opened up the way of salvation to the Gentiles—*inviting them to join Him in becoming His household and body, like He did with the Jews.* Paul also highlighted *his special*

insight into this mystery (v. 4). This refers back to verse 3 regarding the revelation Paul had received directly from God about this mystery.

Of course, Paul made it clear, in verse 5, that other people did not have knowledge of this mystery in *previous generations*. The mystery was not fully revealed by God until some time after Christ's death and resurrection, though there were many hints of it in the Old Testament. Now there is a new strategy in place for God's purposes, or some call this a new *dispensation*. This reinforces the fact that the Old Covenant, with its laws and regulations, has been replaced with the New Covenant, based in Christ's grace and forgiveness. The Spirit of God revealed this mystery to the *New Testament* apostles and prophets. So this could mean that Paul's reference to *"apostles and prophets,"* in 3:20, was a reference strictly to the apostles and prophets who lived in New Testament times.

Verse 6 is packed full of amazing truths and inspiring promises fulfilled. This mystery of Christ involves sharing the gospel with the Gentiles so that they can become heirs together with Israel. *Now* both groups are united through faith in Christ —being *"heirs together, members together of one body and sharers together in the promise in Christ."* As a Christ-follower, I inherit what Christ inherits, since I am a co-heir of His glorious inheritance (Rom. 8:17). I am also a member of Christ's body, which means that I'm intimately connected to and a part of Him; *and you are too, if you're a Christ-follower.* We also must remember that this concept of being part of Christ's body changed the way the Jewish converts viewed themselves—transforming it from separate and superior to the Gentiles, *to being family through Christ.* Most importantly, every Christ-follower shares the same promise as the Jews of salvation through Christ. It is a privilege and honor that now belongs to every believer, no matter your race or nationality. *Christ is the great Unifier . . . Mystery solved!*

Thought to take:

I'm moved by this reading to fully realize the wonder and beauty of Christ's love. Jesus didn't want to leave any Gentile out of His heavenly home, nor to keep His glorious riches from them. He did this because His love is so powerful and overwhelming that it knocks down and destroys every barrier in His path. This is such a mysterious concept to the world, as well as to my human heart. But through Christ and His word, I'm beginning to understand and see the glory that His mystery contains. So that's where my mind will rest—*in this glorious mystery*—as well as wrestling with its profound and jaw-dropping meaning all day long and all life long.

T2t: Rest in and wrestle with God's mystery

Help: Pray for God's help to apply your T2t both now and all day long.

Father, I want to understand more deeply and intimately this mystery You have revealed and fulfilled through Christ. So help me to apply these truths from Your word, as well as communing with You all throughout this day. Also open my eyes to see more of this mystery as I go about my day—seeing how it impacts and blesses me, especially when faced with challenges and temptations. I'm grateful not only for Your salvation, but also for the inheritance Christ shares with me. You include me as part of Christ's body and give me every spiritual blessing I could ever want or need through Your Son. May I reflect on Your love and acceptance when I am tempted to feel discouraged or insecure—yielding to its encouraging truth and *barrier-busting power*. In Jesus' name, amen.

Yield: Surrender yourself to God and His truths—reflecting on and applying your T2t all day long.

18 - THE POOR AND LOWLY MADE RICH

Week 4, Day 3—*Ephesians 3:7-9*

Welcome the Lord: Ask Him to reveal His truth to you as you study.

Observe what the Scripture says:
7 - I became a servant of this gospel by the gift of God's grace given me through the working of his power.
8 - Although I am less than the least of all the Lord's people, this grace was given me: to preach to the Gentiles the boundless riches of Christ,
9 - and to make plain to everyone the administration of this mystery, which for ages past was kept hidden in God, who created all things.

Recognize what is noteworthy and true:
In verse 7, Paul referred to himself as a *"servant"* or some translations say *"minister."* The actual Greek word used by Paul was *"diakonos,"* which refers to a servant who is constantly at the beck and call of his boss. It seems that Paul wanted people to recognize his complete submission to the Lord, as well as his eagerness to bend low in service to them. He considered this calling to be a *"gift of God's grace."* This was quite the paradoxical statement, considering the fact that Paul was a high-ranking Pharisee before coming to the Lord. Paul viewed this gift of grace to be of *greater value* than his former position, even though it left him in a lowly servant's role.

Paul went on (v. 8) to speak in very humble and contrite ways about himself—making it clear that he believed he was an unlikely candidate to receive God's grace. However, since grace is *unmerited favor*, no one deserves this gift from God. Grace by its nature is miraculously endowed, *not earned*. But I'm sure Paul felt it was undeserved for him, because he had persecuted and ordered the killing of many Christians before his own conversion. So to be given this chance to preach the *"boundless riches of Christ"* to the Gentiles, must have felt like a huge honor. I'm sure he realized that every bit of the wealth he had gained when he was a Pharisee paled in comparison to the riches of knowing Christ.

In verse 9, Paul understood that his calling was to *"make plain"* the administration of this mystery. The Greek word used here for *"make plain"* is *"phōtisai"*—*meaning to shine a light on.* Certainly the gospel illuminates God's plan of salvation in every Christ-follower's heart and mind. The *"administration"* of this mystery is translated in some other translations as *"fellowship"* of the mystery, which indicates that God wants to reveal this mystery to both the Jews *and* the Gentiles. After the *"mystery"* was revealed to us and our faith was placed in Christ, we could *plainly* see and understand all the boundless riches God provides —*Gentiles not excluded.*

God had hidden these riches for ages, but now *(by the time of this writing)* they were revealed to Paul and the other apostles. It was as if God had been holding these riches in a secret vault and He finally opened the door for these *"ministers"* to come inside and gaze upon the glittering and heavenly mystery of Christ. Paul could not and would not keep this mystery to himself. He was compelled and called by God to preach this mystery about the New Covenant—*founded in grace*—inviting Gentiles to join with the Jewish believers in receiving Christ's salvation.

Thought to take:
I want to remember just how rich Christ has made me through

my salvation and inheritance in Him. If God's Spirit could take Paul from being a persecutor of the church, of Christ, as well as an arrogant and legalistic Pharisee, to a man humble and completely devoted to Christ, then I know without a doubt how miraculous Christ's salvation is! I will meditate all throughout this day on the riches Christ gives me through His salvation. I also will choose to be a humble servant to Him, including serving those I encounter all throughout this day.

T2t: Humbly serve God and others

Help: Pray for God's help to apply your T2t both now and all day long.

Father, just like the Apostle Paul, I am a servant of the gospel and have been endowed with Your amazing grace. So keep me from shirking my calling or pulling back from the task at hand. There are too many people in my life that need to know and receive the boundless riches of Christ for me to sit back or leave this job up to others. I also realize that there is no guarantee of tomorrow, so I must make the most of every day and opportunity, knowing that it might be my last or the last moment for the ones I speak to today. And as I approach this calling and task, may I do so in a humble and gentle spirit, like Paul always maintained. This will ensure that those I encounter see Christ's gentle and servant-hearted attitude shining through me. For there is no task You ask me to do that is too lowly or difficult, since Your Spirit is stronger in my weakness and submission than at any other time. Give me the ability to yield in a spiritual free-fall into Your gracious arms today! In Jesus' name, amen.

Yield: Surrender yourself to God and His truths—reflecting on and applying your T2t all day long.

19 - VIEWS FROM AFAR AND UP CLOSE

Week 4, Day 4—Ephesians 3:10-12

Welcome the Lord: Ask Him to reveal His truth to you as you study.

Observe what the Scripture says:
10 - *His intent was that now, through the church, the manifold wisdom of God should be made known to the rulers and authorities in the heavenly realms,*
11 - *according to his eternal purpose that he accomplished in Christ Jesus our Lord.*
12 - *In him and through faith in him we may approach God with freedom and confidence.*

Recognize what is noteworthy and true:
All throughout this chapter, Paul identified the purpose God has for His *"mystery"* (v. 9) that was once revealed only to the Jews, but now has also been revealed to the Gentiles. In yesterday's reading, Paul revealed his part in this revelation to the Gentiles. But today, beginning here, in verse 10, Paul explored God's *intent* behind this mysterious purpose. God was and is using the church—*all Christ-followers, in a corporate sense*—as His display of *"manifold wisdom."* The Greek word for *"manifold"* is *"polupoikilos"* and is literally translated as *"of differing colors."* So in a sense, the church is a rainbow that beams with hues of God's wisdom to a watching spiritual world—*dazzling their eyes*

with colorful light.

Moving further in verse 10, Paul identified that God's wisdom is revealed to the *"rulers and authorities in the heavenly realms."* This begs the question: *Who are the rulers and authorities in the heavenly realms, other than the Godhead?* I immediately think of the angels, and I would be right to think this way. These *"rulers and authorities"* most likely include God's angels, as well as demonic or fallen angels. I recall that in 1 Peter 1:12, Peter talked about how the angels of God love to look into the way the Holy Spirit transforms the lives of believers. Since the angels of God live as pure beings without need for redemption, they must marvel at the way God takes our impurity and brokenness—*miraculously forgiving, binding up, and healing us.* It's like the best reality and redemption show ever, except that our beautiful redemption, *sadly,* will never be a reality for them as angels.

Lest we forget, in verse 11, Paul tied God's intent and vehicle of His wisdom back to His eternal purpose, which is found in and accomplished through Christ. Obviously, what exactly Christ accomplished is our redemption and salvation—*both for the Jew and the Gentile.*

In verse 12, Paul reminded the Ephesian believers, *and us,* that this mystery is only revealed *in and through Christ,* as we place our *faith in Him.* Once we place our faith in Christ, we gain access to God and can *"approach"* Him with both *"freedom and confidence."* It is important to remember that Paul was talking about both the Jew and Gentile having this access to approach God. What had once been anathema was now gloriously resplendent. If that isn't enough for us, as Christ-followers, God gives us boldness and freedom in this new relationship with Him. The Greek meaning behind this idea is that we have complete *freedom of speech* with God. He wants to hear our every concern, regret, doubt, sorrow, as well as what brings us joy and satisfaction. He is the perfect, attentive Parent and/or smitten Bridegroom that every person longs for in this life.

Thought to take:

It is hard for me to choose between two very important take-aways from this reading. The first is to not forget the importance of my role in the corporate body of believers. By that, I don't mean, attending church per se—*though that's certainly important and valuable to my faith walk.* One of the challenges here is to be—*as part of the body of Christ*—God's colorful and multi-faceted demonstration of His wisdom to those in the spiritual realms. The second challenge is to recognize that my relationship with Christ comes with total access to God and the freedom to speak my heart and mind to Him at all times. So I will celebrate with my fellow-believers the wisdom God gives me and rely on the intimate access He grants me.

T2t: Display God's wisdom by turning to Him

Help: Pray for God's help to apply your T2t both now and all day long.

Father, thank You not just for my salvation—*which is immeasurably wondrous*—but also for this family, household and body of faith that I am able to join with in displaying Your mystery. I tend to think about how my salvation is a mystery to those who do not know You; but that's only half of Your audience who eagerly watches Your glory on display. Help me to remember that angels are looking upon this mystery from afar and even up close. They cannot grasp it totally, and neither do I! *But we all marvel at it!* I also thank You for urging me to come near every single minute of my day and share my heart with You as often as possible. What a loving God You are—*to guide and comfort me in every circumstance in my life, so that I might experience Your best and be able to do my best for You.* With that in mind, empower me to live a life each day that displays Your colorful manifold wisdom to all here on earth and beyond! In Jesus' name, amen.

Yield: Surrender yourself to God and His truths—reflecting on and applying your T2t all day long.

20 - PAIN IS WORTH
THE PURPOSE

Week 4, Day 5—Ephesians 3:13-15

Welcome the Lord: Ask Him to reveal His truth to you as you study.

Observe what the Scripture says:
13 - *I ask you, therefore, not to be discouraged because of my sufferings for you, which are your glory.*
14 - *For this reason I kneel before the Father,*
15 - *from whom every family in heaven and on earth derives its name.*

Recognize what is noteworthy and true:
A casual reading of verse 13 might not yield the many gems that are hidden within this verse and passage. So I've done some additional research to understand the context. The suffering that Paul did not want the Ephesian believers *"to be discouraged"* about was a reference to his imprisonment. He was confined to house arrest because of a conflict that is detailed in Acts 22:21ff. The conflict involved believing Jews who hated the idea of the Gentiles being included in God's call to salvation, often vehemently resisted the idea of Christ as the Messiah before coming to the Lord themselves. However, Paul embraced not only Christ's Messiahship, but every part of his call to suffer as being *for the glory* of every Christ-follower—*wanting the Ephesians to feel the same way as well.* Actually, God was able to use Paul *more*

extensively and prominently *because of* his arrest and sufferings for Christ and the church than without it.

In verse 14, there is much that Paul intended and meant in the little phrase, *"For this reason."* That's because Paul was focused on the most important of reasons possible—*devoting His life to Christ and suffering for His sake.* Paul was intent on furthering the gospel to the Gentiles, and encouraging and deepening the faith of all believers who benefitted, *and still benefit*, from his many letters included in the New Testament. His mention of kneeling before the Father gives us a tender portrait of a man fully devoted to God—*humbling himself through this posture in prayer.* From my experience, kneeling before God can do wonders in righting my perspective and attuning my heart to hear my beloved Father's voice. I truly believe it aids me in feeling His presence all around me, as well as reminding me of how desperately and continually I need God's grace.

In verse 15, Paul reminded his audience once again that, as Christ-followers, *we are part of God's family.* As a believer, I derive my name as the Father's child and Jesus' bride, all the while I walk upon the soil of *earth* each day of my life. But this also means that I am part of this heavenly group that will gather one day to worship the Lord as *one big family of God* before His throne. Some commentators believe that the mention of *"every family in heaven"* might be a reference to angels being related to one another through heavenly families, even though Jesus revealed that angels never marry (Mt. 22:29-30). One way or another, there is a great emphasis on the bond we have through Christ. As I reflect on the context of Paul's message here, I also see that Paul's statement about being one family served to remind both the Jew and Gentile believers that they—*and we*—are one through our faith in God's family. No believer is superior to any another, nor excluded from God's grace.

Thought to take:
If I were in Paul's shoes—*imprisoned unjustly*—it would be so

easy for me to become discouraged and feel as if God had abandoned me or at least had lost sight of my plight. This reminds me to embrace my sufferings, like Paul did, knowing that God is faithfully using them to further His purposes. There's a bigger and better story in this life than God relieving my every pain and restriction. How I respond in those injustices are what can help to further God's purposes in my life, as well as other people's lives. So I will reflect on how God has used the suffering in my life to bring about His good—*making it my goal to join Him in that effort.*

T2t: What good has God brought from my pain?

Help: Pray for God's help to apply your T2t both now and all day long.

Father, it is so easy for me to turn my eyes from You and onto the injustices and suffering that I'm experiencing. But that was not the way Paul lived his life. He embraced the pain in each moment, knowing that You were using it to bring about the best result—*not just for himself—but for every Christ-follower.* I am one of those Christ-followers who has benefited from Paul's faith-filled actions and attitudes. So I thank You for his life, and ask that You would help me to live like him, in a way that trusts You completely in my pain and suffering. Deepen my faith through these difficulties—using it to draw me to my knees in prayer. May I fully recognize the power and privilege of entering Your presence with my requests, as well as the requests of my brothers and sisters in Christ. I commit to bending low in prayer and trusting You to bring about Your best in all of our lives. In Jesus' name, amen.

Yield: Surrender yourself to God and His truths—reflecting on and applying your T2t all day long.

Week Four Group Discussion Questions

3:1-3—God Lets Us in on His Secret

What do you think *"chaining yourself"* to Jesus might involve and require?

3:4-6—Rest in and Wrestle with God

What are some things that might keep believers from embracing their oneness with other believers? What might help us to lay our hindrances at Christ's feet?

3:7-9—The Poor and Lowly Made Rich

What hesitancies keep believers from embracing the riches Christ offers them? In what ways do you hesitate to embrace Christ's riches or His calling on your life?

3:10-12—Views from Afar and Up Close

What are some ways we can display God's wisdom more brightly? How does it feel to know God wants you to come to Him in freedom and confidence?

3:13-15—Pain is Worth the Purpose

What painful experience in your life has God used to highlight His grace and goodness, and in what way? What are some ways we can pray for other believers?

21 - A LOVE THAT FILLS EVERY CREVICE

Week 5, Day 1—Ephesians 3:16-18

Welcome the Lord: Ask Him to reveal His truth to you as you study.

Observe what the Scripture says:
16 - *I pray that out of his glorious riches he may strengthen you with power through his Spirit in your inner being,*
17 - *so that Christ may dwell in your hearts through faith. And I pray that you, being rooted and established in love,*
18 - *may have power, together with all the Lord's holy people, to grasp how wide and long and high and deep is the love of Christ.*

Recognize what is noteworthy and true:
What a sweet way to begin the reading today here in verse 16—*with Paul's heartfelt prayer for these believers!* He began by asking that the Lord would strengthen them out of His *"glorious riches."* When I think about how rich the Lord truly is—*being the Creator, Owner and Sovereign Manager of all that there is on earth and throughout the heavens*—I realize the depth and potential of this prayer. But it's important to hone in on the riches that *"strengthen"* believers with the Spirit's power in our *"inner being."* Paul wasn't talking about monetary or earthly riches, but rather spiritual, eternal and infinite blessings that saturate and fill us to overflowing from within. When I reflect on and praise God for these riches, I feel God strengthening me. And it is a prayer that I'm inspired to pray for other believers as well.

In verse 17, Paul wanted the Spirit's power to invade and dwell in the hearts of these believers through their faith in Christ. If they were already Christ-followers, that would mean he was praying that they would *welcome* Christ as the Resident and Landlord of their heart and life. This would also mean living out their salvation in ways that reflect a growing relationship with Christ. If they were not believers yet, I believe this would be a prayer for each person to allow Christ access to their hearts through faith in Christ's salvation. Either way, Paul wanted these people—*and us too*—to allow Christ to have complete access to our hearts from the point of our salvation onward.

Paul further backed this up when he prayed for them to be *"rooted and established in love"* (v. 18). I find it interesting that he said to be established in *"love,"* rather than in God's word or truth. It seems his emphasis was on believers loving the Lord so that they are able to love each other with the love of the Lord. This also means that every Christ-follower has power that can only be tapped into by *joining together* in Christ's love for each other. Furthermore, it is only through the act of loving God, receiving God's love, and extending it to our brothers and sisters in Christ that we can truly *grasp* how wide, long, high and deep Christ's love is. Finally, it sounds as if Christ's love can be measured—*even though it is infinite and incomprehensible*. In enduringword.com, David Guzik said of this phenomenon, *"God's love is wide enough to include every person. God's love is long enough to last through all eternity. God's love is deep enough to reach the worst sinner. God's love is high enough to take us to heaven."* Amazingly, Christ's love meets our deepest need from every angle and direction possible.

Thought to take:
Even though Paul prayed this prayer ages ago, I still feel encouraged by his words whenever I read this passage. It feels as if God continues to listen to Paul's prayer—*answering it every time we read and take these words to heart in our present day and time.* But

what I'm most inspired by is the need to send down roots by establishing myself in God's love, as well as joining with other believers to live out our love for Christ *together.* Therefore, I will rest in the truth that God loves me. I will then extend His love to others, especially with those in the family of faith. And I will find ways to join with my brothers and sisters in Christ, sharing God's love in miraculous ways to everyone we meet.

T2t: Receive and extend God's love

Help: Pray for God's help to apply your T2t both now and all day long.

Father, I feel as if I cannot pray a prayer any better than the Apostle Paul prayed for the Ephesians. I want the same things for my brothers and sisters in Christ, as Paul did in his day. So I pray that You would honor my plea for Your rich strength to be poured upon the heads of all who have been adopted into Your divine family. Allow this power to penetrate every crevice and corner of my inner being, as well as into the hearts of my godly friends. May this result in Christ gaining access to all that is within each of us. And I, for one, do not want to hold anything in reserve—*surrendering it all to You*—so that You can be strong in my weaknesses. Help me to gain a greater grasp of Your love by first seeking Your love, reveling in Your love, and then extending Your love to every person I come in contact with this day. May the whole world see and experience Your boundless love in real and tangible ways in and through my life. In Jesus' name, amen.

Yield: Surrender yourself to God and His truths—reflecting on and applying your T2t all day long.

22 - BE FILLED SO WE CAN SPILL

Week 5, Day 2—*Ephesians 3:19-21*

Welcome the Lord: Ask Him to reveal His truth to you as you study.

Observe what the Scripture says:
19 - *and to know this love that surpasses knowledge—that you may be filled to the measure of all the fullness of God.*
20 - *Now to him who is able to do immeasurably more than all we ask or imagine, according to his power that is at work within us,*
21 - *to him be glory in the church and in Christ Jesus throughout all generations, for ever and ever! Amen.*

Recognize what is noteworthy and true:
Even though I'm entering today's reading mid-sentence (v. 19), I see where Paul has taken this prayer. He wanted the Ephesian believers—*and us by extension*—to know the love of God. I find it interesting that Paul did not pray for believers to *feel* this love, though we certainly can and will as we receive God's love. However, Paul's emphasis here was on *knowing* God's love, which *surpasses* our human knowledge. *How can we know what is unknowable?* Only by seeking God's love through His word and prayer, and then letting His love flow in and out of us in loving interactions each day.

In the latter part of verse 19, Paul prayed that believers would be filled to the measure of *all the fullness of God.* Each person is filled with God's Spirit at the point of salvation, but there is more that Christ-followers should strive for as we go along in our faith walk. Paul was praying that believers be filled to the utmost level with *all the fullness of God.* This is too great a result to really measure; yet Paul endeavored to point out the bulls-eye of where our ambitions and affections should be aimed each day. The target and focus for our hearts should be God in *all of His fullness.*

In verse 20, Paul turned his focus from praying for the saints, to addressing and praising the Lord for the work He always does in His children's lives. I also note that Paul continued with references to *measurements*—saying God is able to do *immeasurably* more than all we ask for or imagine in this life. Paul called it like it is. Even though he has *(and we have)* attempted to quantify the Lord and His power, it is truly *immeasurable—going beyond what we could ever imagine or do on our own.* This immeasurable, infinite and incomprehensible power is at work within every believer *today.* And this is not just when we enter God's presence in eternity. I think I only allow God to work an infinitesimal fraction of what He could be doing in my life each day, if only I trusted and yielded to Him more.

In verse 21, it's interesting that Paul did not ask for the Lord to receive glory in his singular life, but instead asked that the Lord be glorified in the *"church."* He might have realized that all the fullness of God cannot be contained in one singular soul, but rather in the *collective hearts* of all believers joining together in God's love. This is when something truly miraculous occurs, and is the best way to glorify Christ throughout every generation. We become the flesh and blood, living and breathing, bodily manifestation of God's love to a *love-hungry* world.

Thought to take:

One main thought that I see from this reading is to let all the fullness of Christ fill up my heart, especially as I join with other believers in letting His fullness and love spill out on the world.

So I will first ask the Lord to reveal anything that has gotten in the way of His work in my life or taken up space in my heart. Then I will surrender those sins and allow Him to take up every bit of territory in my heart and life. I will pray that other believers join me in this emptying of self and filling up of Jesus.

T2t: Give Jesus more room in my heart

Help: Pray for God's help to apply your T2t both now and all day long.

Father, I want to know this love that surpasses my own human knowledge and understanding. Even though I cannot comprehend Your love, I know that I can be filled up with more of You, as I yield my heart more completely to Your care and power. Enable me to give You greater access to flow in and through my heart—going on to do even more unfathomable miracles in my life. Reveal to me those areas that I hold in reserve, and grant me the strength and willingness to release them at Your feet. For I know that when I let go, You will pour into my open hand more and more of Your love and presence. It will fill up my heart in ways that bless and draw others to You. I lift up my brothers and sisters in Christ, trusting that You will fill them to overflowing with Your love and presence as well. Use us like a mighty ocean of love breaking forth on everyone in this world —immersing all in Your amazing grace and love. In Jesus' name, amen.

Yield: Surrender yourself to God and His truths—reflecting on and applying your T2t all day long.

23 - BIND MY HEART
TO JESUS

Week 5, Day 3—Ephesians 4:1-3

Welcome the Lord: Ask Him to reveal His truth to you as you study.

Observe what the Scripture says:
1 - As a prisoner for the Lord, then, I urge you to live a life worthy of the calling you have received.
2 - Be completely humble and gentle; be patient, bearing with one another in love.
3 - Make every effort to keep the unity of the Spirit through the bond of peace.

Recognize what is noteworthy and true:
Paul turned his focus from a prayer about all that God has given believers (in the previous chapter) to instructions here, *beginning in verse 1*, about what Christ-followers should be willing to do for our generous God. Some translations begin verse 1 with *"therefore,"* which helps to link the message in chapter 3 with what Paul began to teach here in chapter 4. Additionally, I notice that Paul identified himself as a *"prisoner for the Lord,"* rather than a prisoner of the Roman Government—especially since he would not have been in that position, *if it were not for his allegiance to God above all.*

With Paul's situation and sacrifice clearly noted, he was able to effectively urge these believers—*and us by extension*—to live lives worthy of the calling we have received from Christ. This perspective and understanding about God's goodness was what gave Paul the ability and desire to submit to imprisonment. I, too, realize that I cannot live a life that is worthy of my calling as a Christ-follower unless I constantly bear in mind just how loving and good my Savior is and has always been to me.

Verse 2 is packed with important character standards for every believer. These were the hallmarks of Christ's life. Therefore, they stand as a way to reflect our worthiness through our relationship with Him. The first two that Paul noted here were the need to be completely "*humble*" and "*gentle*." A better translation of humble might be "*lowliness*" or even "*humiliation*." We must be willing to bend low in submission to God and others, *even to the point of humiliation.* Humbleness was certainly on display as Paul willingly humbled himself to an unjust imprisonment. And it took gentleness to accept this harsh and humiliating plight as well. I'm sure the Roman guards were astonished daily by Paul's gentle attitude.

The next two attributes that Paul encouraged all believers to pursue were patience and a love that perseveres under attack and trial. Both of these qualities dovetail one another, since both patience and a love that bears up under suffering involve staying true to the Lord. I find that I can only endure in times of loss and unfairness when I stay focused on sacrificing *for the Lord.*

Paul linked the idea in verse 2—"*love for one another*"—with verse 3, urging believers to make every effort to "*keep the unity of the Spirit.*" When we are unified with the Spirit, love will flow. Paul also linked unity to the "*bond of peace*" found in Christ. Interestingly, Paul began this chapter identifying himself as a *prisoner* for the Lord, which also involves a *bond.* However, this bond is sweet, since it wraps up every believer tightly, unifying us with one another and the Lord. These are chains and bonds that are pleasant, reassuring and bring us "*peace.*" This is not just a peace that we individually enjoy, but is made more powerful and obvious in the family of God—being unified through the

Prince of Peace!

Thought to take:

I may not be imprisoned like Paul was here, but I face situations that feel confining and unfair nearly every day. I can easily let those define, distract and discourage me in my day-to-day walk with God. But after studying today's passage, I realize that I don't have to let those things define me, *but rather refine me as a prisoner of Christ!* So I will recalibrate my focus from my confining circumstances over to my humble, gentle and loving Savior. It is then that I know I'll be able to gain the bond of peace that not only binds my heart to His, but to every other believer as well.

T2t: Be humble, gentle and loving like Christ

Help: Pray for God's help to apply your T2t both now and all day long.

Father, it's so easy to let the unfair circumstances I face in life imprison me—chaining me to the lie that I am without help and hope. But You have saved me from the chains of my sin—*calling me out of that life and into a life that is worthy of Your Son's name.* So in every tempting moment today, encourage me to view each difficulty through the lens of my calling. And inspire me to endure suffering for Christ's sake alone. May that result in a life that brings greater honor and glory to You because I'm choosing to be humble and gentle, as well as patient and loving with others. Use this yielded posture to draw me closer to others, in particular to my brothers and sisters in Christ. Create an incredible bond in our lives that reflects the love and peace of the *Prince of Peace*—our Lord Jesus Christ. In Your Son's name, amen.

Yield: Surrender yourself to God and His truths—reflecting on and applying your T2t all day long.

24 - 'ONE' IN THE ONE AND ONLY

***Week 5, Day 4**—Ephesians 4:4-6*

Welcome the Lord: Ask Him to reveal His truth to you as you study.

Observe what the Scripture says:
4 - *There is one body and one Spirit, just as you were called to one hope when you were called;*
5 - *one Lord, one faith, one baptism;*
6 - *one God and Father of all, who is over all and through all and in all.*

Recognize what is noteworthy and true:
Paul continued to talk, here in verse 4, about the *"bond"* (v. 3) and oneness every Christ-follower experiences through Christ. As the *"body"* of Christ, we cannot and should not be fractured by our own independent wills. Our singular part in the family of God is never as important as when we join with the whole. The only way believers can be unified in this way is through the *"one Spirit"*—who calls us to *"one hope."* This *one hope* is found and known only in and through the hope of salvation.

In verse 5, Paul went on to identify where this salvation comes from—it comes from our *"one Lord"* Jesus Christ. Paul then identified how we gain this salvation . It is through the vehicle of our *"one faith"* in Christ. There is no other means by which we can be saved, except to reach out in faith and trust that God will flood and cleanse our hearts with His forgiveness and redemption. As Christ-followers, we may not always agree with each other on the non-essentials of our faith, but the essential—*faith in Christ*—can and will always be what binds us together.

Paul went further to describe the next step in the believer's faith walk—saying that we are united in and called to *"one baptism."* Paul was not saying there's only one mode or type of baptism here. His emphasis was on the cleansing and regeneration that the Spirit does within our hearts at the point of salvation. There are several verses in Scripture that speak of the baptism of the Holy Spirit that, *I believe*, takes place at the point of faith in Christ. This means *water baptism* is distinct in that it is an outward symbol of this inner transformation done by the Holy Spirit, when the Spirit comes to inhabit and baptize our hearts as believers (Mt. 3:11, Acts 1:5 and 11:16).

Moving on to verse 6, I think it's important to stop and reflect on the context of each *"one"* that Paul listed here. For example, Paul had good reason to point out to these Jewish and Gentile believers that they were *"one"* with each other through the various aspects of their faith in their *"one God and Father."* The Jewish believers at this time were tempted to view the new Gentile converts as inferior or not truly their family in Christ. But the fact is, no difference in methodology or race can disrupt the oneness we enjoy through our *one God* and *one faith* in Christ.

Further down in verse 6, Paul did not leave any aspect of our faith in Christ up for question or debate. He wanted to unpack exactly how the Lord permeates within us as His body and family. The Lord is *"over all,"* just like the roof of a building brings shelter and shade for our protection and care. Being *"over all"* also reminds us of His great authority over us, as His body, but also over every other authority on earth and in the spiritual realms. The Lord is also *"through all"*—most likely meaning working through all who come to Him in faith. Finally, the Lord is *"in all"*—meaning *in* every believer, since the Spirit dwells *within* those who place their faith in Christ alone.

Thought to take:

Only in the mysterious truths of God can we find that one plus one plus one plus one plus one plus one plus one *(one body, one Spirit, one hope, one Lord, one faith, one baptism, one God/Father —seven in total!)* still equals one! I want to remember that it's only through my faith in the Lord that I am able to be one not only with Him, but also with all believers who place their faith in Him. This truth compels me to respond with Christ's love and acceptance of my fellow Christians, since we are one in His body.

T2t: Be one with Christ and other believers

Help: Pray for God's help to apply your T2t both now and all day long.

Father, what a mystery and miracle-maker You are! For the unfolding of this mystery confounds me, yet also provides great comfort and clarity of purpose found only in You. So let me recount all the many ways that You make me one with You and Your body through Your one and only Son. Help me to yield to Your Spirit's work in my life today, as well as accepting and loving those who share this oneness through our faith in You. For it is no secret how often I feel the pull to make *my* choices based on my own preferences and independent will, when You desire for me to align myself with You, as well as with Your sons and daughters in Christ. Make my life reflect this singular purpose, helping me to come alongside the family of faith, so that the world will know we are one in Your bond of love and peace. In Christ's name, amen.

Yield: Surrender yourself to God and His truths—reflecting on and applying your T2t all day long.

25 - NO PLACE IS UNTOUCHED BY CHRIST

***Week 5, Day 5**—Ephesians 4:7-10*

Welcome the Lord: Ask Him to reveal His truth to you as you study.

Observe what the Scripture says:
7 - *But to each one of us grace has been given as Christ apportioned it.*
8 - *This is why it says: "When he ascended on high, he took many captives and gave gifts to his people."*
9 - *(What does "he ascended" mean except that he also descended to the lower, earthly regions?*
10 - *He who descended is the very one who ascended higher than all the heavens, in order to fill the whole universe.)*

Recognize what is noteworthy and true:
Today's reading is obviously one that begs for deeper insight and study. However in verse 7 Paul was rather straightforward about this grace given to each believer *"as Christ apportioned it."* But I'm left wondering: *What type of grace was he talking about, and in what way is it apportioned?* I looked to the context for clues and found that the verses following today's reading reflect the grace of God demonstrated through the various spiritual gifts—given and begun when a believer receives *saving grace.* The fact that this grace is measured or apportioned to each believer by the discretion of Christ, also leads me to see this as

grace in the form of spiritual gifts. I take that view because foundationally every believer receives the same and sufficient amount of *saving grace* at the moment our faith is placed in Christ.

I find verse 8 to be a bit murkier and feel like it cannot be deciphered by looking *only* at the context. First off, I note that Paul loosely quoted the Psalmist's prophecy (Ps. 68:18) about Christ's *ascension* after His resurrection to heaven. I believe the mention of *"captives"* here refers to how every person has been held captive by sin and death. However, Christ, as Savior and Deliverer, removed the curse of sin and death through His triumph over the grave (1 Cor. 15:55-57). It's not exactly clear what was meant by the idea of Christ giving *gifts to His people*. But, if these gifts refer to spiritual gifts, then the thought aligns well with the gifts Paul went on to innumerate in tomorrow's reading, verses 11-12.

In verse 9, Paul then moved backwards from Christ's *ascension* to mentioning how Christ *"descended to the lower, earthly regions."* It is noteworthy to mention that some think this idea refers to an event mentioned in 1 Peter 3:19 and 4:6 that reveals how Christ preached to the *spirits in prison.* No one knows for sure exactly who those spirits were, though many theologians speculate on various options. I will refrain from doing so, since it is not necessary for a proper application of today's text.

In verse 10, Paul continued to be a bit cryptic about all that transpired during Christ's mission to save the lost. Nevertheless, I see that the main point here is to recognize the depth to which Christ went to complete His mission of salvation. There is no piece or part of our *"universe,"* nor experience, that Christ has not conquered and brought into submission to His will by the power of His redeeming blood. He fills up our every gap and need we have in this life with His power and dominion over sin and death. Therefore, we are *"captives"* (v. 8) set free by His saving power and grace.

Thought to take:

This reading moves me to remember and integrate the truth and idea of Christ going to every possible region in the universe to complete His mission to save and free my soul. This reminds me of Psalm 139:7-10—knowing that God is inescapable and always near me no matter where I might go. This can be both comforting and disconcerting, depending on how yielded my heart is to Him in any given moment. But today, I will view and embrace it as a comforting reality in my day.

T2t: Remember how *far* Jesus went for me

Help: Pray for God's help to apply your T2t both now and all day long.

Dear Jesus, thank You for the many grace gifts You have given me, as well as to every person You have redeemed. I'm so thankful that You not only chose to save my soul and free me from sin, but that You also wanted each member of Your body to operate with holy powers and wiring that You alone could infuse and awake within us. Help me to respond to and welcome this grace that stirs and courses within my heart each day. May I find opportunities to give this grace to others as You have given to me. Use my efforts to bless all that I come in contact with today and every day. And help me to always remember how high and low, as well as deep and wide You went to save my soul. This truth comforts me, for I know that I am *never alone—Your Spirit is always near no matter where I might roam.* So I will praise You all throughout this day for that wonderful gift of salvation, won by You, my victorious Savior. In Your name, amen.

Yield: Surrender yourself to God and His truths—reflecting on and applying your T2t all day long.

Week Five Group Discussion Questions

3:16-18—A Love that Fills Every Crevice

Which of these four areas are you strongest/weakest in, and why? How would you rate yourself (1 to 10) on grasping the magnitude of Christ's love?

3:19-21—Be Filled So We Can Spill

What is one way God has shown you love that was/is beyond your expectations or imagination? How can you share the love of God with others in your life?

4:1-3—Bind My Heart to Jesus

Which of the godly character qualities, listed in Ephesians 4:1-3, is weakest in your life? What is one action you can take to improve that particular attribute in your life?

4:4-6—'One' in the One and Only

What are some ways you have let your individuality interfere with your oneness with God and other believers? How can you change that approach and rest in the oneness found in Christ?

4:7-10—No Place is Untouched by Christ

What does knowing how far Jesus went for you inspire you to do and/or think? Pray together as a group for each of these desires and aims today!

26 - FINDING CHRIST'S FULLNESS

Week 6, Day 1—Ephesians 4:11-13

Welcome the Lord: Ask Him to reveal His truth to you as you study.

Observe what the Scripture says:
11 - *So Christ himself gave the apostles, the prophets, the evangelists, the pastors and teachers,*
12 - *to equip his people for works of service, so that the body of Christ may be built up*
13 - *until we all reach unity in the faith and in the knowledge of the Son of God and become mature, attaining to the whole measure of the fullness of Christ.*

Recognize what is noteworthy and true:
Beginning here in verse 11, Paul identified some of the various grace gifts (vv. 7-8) that Christ gives to certain members of His body for the building up (v. 12) of the body of believers. However, the emphasis is not on the *"gift"* per se, but on the offices that Christ established through these gifts given to certain people. Therefore, some are/were called to the office of apostle, some to the office of prophet, evangelist or pastor-teacher. The Greek term here for *"pastor and teacher"* describes more of a dual role within one office—*thus, pastor-teacher is the clearest translation.*

Each office had and has specific duties. The office of an apostle is to be a special ambassador of God's word. However, *modern-day apostles* do not possess the same authority as the apostles of that former day and time. A good example of an apostle in our modern times would be a church-planter or missionary. The office of a prophet is to accurately speak or preach God's word. Prophets during Paul's day and age were given more authority than modern-day prophets, since they were the ones Christ built His church upon (Eph. 2:20). The office of an evangelist is specific to preaching the gospel both in *and outside* of the church. The office of pastor-teacher is one of shepherding and leading those within the church, as well as teaching and instructing them in God's word.

In verse 12, Paul gave the reason these four main offices within a church body were established—*to equip God's people for "works of service."* These offices or *officers* that Christ instituted provide the training and support necessary for those within the church to go out and share the gospel with others, and to minister in the ways that reflect Christ's love. I take this to mean that I am able to build up Christ's body every time I serve. I'm also reminded that every believer plays as important of a role in Christ's plan as the leaders do in our churches and communities, since we all build up the body of Christ.

Paul fleshed out (v. 13) what our service as believers *more specifically* achieves. First of all, we achieve *unity* when we function in this way. Our work stems from the unity we share in our faith in Christ. But this cannot be sustained unless we are also growing in our *"knowledge of the Son of God."* As we come to know God better, we do *more than grow older* in our faith, we *"mature"* in our faith. I also see that the concept of measurement was inserted here again in the latter part of verse 13, which seems to circle back to the measurements Paul spoke of in regards to Christ in verses 8-10. If Christ went to every *extent and length* to save our souls, *then shouldn't we strive to go to every length to become more and more like Him?* It is then that we can become not just Christ-like, *but full of Christ as well!* That's the measuring rod I want to measure myself against each day!

Thought to take:
One main thought from this reading is the need to play my part in building up the church. I may not be called to be an apostle, prophet, evangelist, or pastor, but I can be someone who grows more spiritually mature under the leaders of my church's teaching and shepherding. So I will take all their spiritual tools and biblical insights and use them in my own studies of God's word —*coming to know the Lord better because of this continual pursuit.* I want to let God's truths permeate every part of my heart and perspective, growing into maturity in my faith. I also know that when I do this, I am helping to build up the body of Christ.

T2t: Find ways to grow in my faith

Help: Pray for God's help to apply your T2t both now and all day long.

Father, I am so grateful for the people Your Son has equipped with gifts that support my church, and ministries beyond my church's walls. I've experienced and been blessed by their ministry first-hand. I would not know *You,* if it weren't for faithful church leaders who have served me in my life. I would not know how to serve others like Christ served me, without the example these pastors and teachers You have set before me. Thank You for their influence, support, and guidance! I also pray that I would take seriously my spiritual growth and service to *You* each day. I know that I must pursue You and Your word so that I can reflect not just a Christ-like attitude but demonstrate the fullness of *Christ* as well. Use this to build a godly legacy pointing others to You and Your love each and every day. In Jesus' name, amen.

Yield: Surrender yourself to God and His truths—reflecting on and applying your T2t all day long.

27 - HOW SPIRITUALLY MATURE AM I?

Week 6, Day 2—Ephesians 4:14-16

Welcome the Lord: Ask Him to reveal His truth to you as you study.

Observe what the Scripture says:

14 - *Then we will no longer be infants, tossed back and forth by the waves, and blown here and there by every wind of teaching and by the cunning and craftiness of people in their deceitful scheming.*
15 - *Instead, speaking the truth in love, we will grow to become in every respect the mature body of him who is the head, that is, Christ.*
16 - *From him the whole body, joined and held together by every supporting ligament, grows and builds up in love, as each part does its work.*

Recognize what is noteworthy and true:

In verse 14, Paul spoke of the reasons why we need to grow into maturity in our faith. As we grow in our faith, we are no longer unsteady and easily toppled like *"infants"* tend to be when they are learning to walk. If we grow into maturity, we also won't be like the waves of the sea that are constantly tossed back and forth by every wind. The *"wind"* represents the doctrines of cunning and crafty people who might use deceitful scheming to try and knock us off course in life. It might be tempting to think that *movement* of any kind is a good thing; but based on this reading, it is clear that we should guard against that lie. Christ's plan is for the leaders of our churches to guide us in right and godly paths, so that we are all *moving in the right direction* of God's truth and love.

In verse 15, Paul revealed one prime way to grow into maturity in our faith—*we are to "speak the truth in love."* Being able to do this comes only as we gain maturity, security and understanding. A young child typically only speaks the truth in ways that can draw attention to his or her need. A teenager might speak the truth in ways that serve to hurt others, so that the teen can feel superior and protect his or her own heart. But mature and secure adults know they must put aside their own agendas and speak about matters of truth in loving ways. Maturity teaches us that caring for others is more important than trying to protect ourselves. Christ was a perfect example of this balance between truth and love—*demonstrating this in the sacrifice of His life for ours.*

Moving further, Paul draws our attention back to the metaphor of the body of Christ—specifically Christ as our *"head."* As the body of Christ, we are to grow into maturity, so that our *"head"—who is Christ*—is our constant focus and aim. This reminds me that my maturity in my faith is not achieved through self-effort, or by making myself the focus and benefactor of my growth—*though I certainly do benefit when I grow in Christ.* My main focus for spiritual growth should be to bring honor to *Christ* and to grow into Him, which enables me to *reflect the face of Christ* to others.

The metaphor continues to unfold in verse 16—reminding us that it is only *"in Him"* that we, as a body, can find unity, grow in our faith, and be built up in and by His love. When, we as believers, turn our energies, priorities and focus completely toward Christ and *His love*, our body functions as it should, *and not as independent and disjointed body parts.*

Thought to take:
I feel as if Paul has provided something of a litmus test for

knowing how mature you and I are in our faith. So I will ask myself: *Am I easily knocked off my feet by the challenges and unfairness in my life, instead of trusting that God is at work to redeem my situation and refine me in the process? Am I letting the beliefs, attitudes and even teachings of others distract and deceive me, instead of remaining faithful to and trusting in God's truths?* If I am easily toppled or distracted, then I can know that I am not nearly as mature as I should be. So I will evaluate myself today based on this *"test"* and recommit myself to knowing, as well as living out and *exercising* God's truth and love. When I make these mature choices, the world will see a clearer picture of the face and love of Christ.

T2t: Test and improve my spiritual maturity

Help: Pray for God's help to apply your T2t both now and all day long.

Father, I come to You totally convinced that I am more easily tossed and blown about in my faith walk than I should be by this point. This message today convicts me to my core, and reinvigorates my desire to turn away from the people and things in this life that distract and deceive me—including my own selfish thoughts and ambitions. You are the only One who holds and embodies pure truth and love. So teach me to throw myself into Your loving embrace whenever I am tempted to go in another direction. Use each crisis of faith in my life to grow me toward spiritual maturity—going further to strengthen my unity with other believers as well. Draw all people to You, as we live out Your love as Christ-following communities and, most importantly, as a *family* of faith. In Christ's name, amen.

Yield: Surrender yourself to God and His truths—reflecting on and applying your T2t all day long.

28 - WHAT HARDENS OUR HEARTS

Week 6, Day 3—*Ephesians 4:17-19*

Welcome the Lord: Ask Him to reveal His truth to you as you study.

Observe what the Scripture says:

17 - *So I tell you this, and insist on it in the Lord, that you must no longer live as the Gentiles do, in the futility of their thinking.*

18 - *They are darkened in their understanding and separated from the life of God because of the ignorance that is in them due to the hardening of their hearts.*

19 - *Having lost all sensitivity, they have given themselves over to sensuality so as to indulge in every kind of impurity and they are full of greed.*

Recognize what is noteworthy and true:

Paul came out swinging here in verse 17—*insisting* on the Ephesian believers no longer living like the *Gentiles*, in the *"futility of their thinking."* This might have insulted the Gentile believers in this church. Still, to many in the church, a Gentile's way of life represented the polar opposite of what Christianity should look like. For a more current day example, it was like Paul saying believers should no longer live or operate like members of the porn industry or like drug addicts. It becomes obvious then that people who exemplify those beliefs and actions are in opposition to Christianity. Paul went further to make the point that *"Gentiles"* often embraced futile or vain thinking—meaning they pursued things that left them empty and longing for more. This is a far cry from how believers can or *should* operate.

In verse 18, Paul offered more descriptors of the Gentile's way of thinking and relating. The Gentile's understanding about life was darkened because they were operating each day out of spiritual blindness. They did not have the light of Jesus to open their eyes to truth, love and hope. Paul then said that Gentiles were *"separated from the life of God."* Those, like Gentiles *(unbelievers)*, who continue in this spiritual blindness, are essentially hardening their hearts to God and His influence on their lives. To do so—*long ago and today*—is to remain comfortable with human ignorance, rather than gaining divine insight and wisdom. Believers are in the Light, while unbelievers remain in the dark.

In verse 19, Paul went from pronouncing that *"Gentiles"* grow ignorant and develop *hard hearts*, to saying they lose *sensitivity* or feeling. Sin has a way of hardening our hearts and erecting walls that separate us not just from God, but also from others in our lives. The longer we live behind these walls we've built with *sin upon sin*, the less we feel the impact our sin has on others—*including God*. This leads to a vicious cycle, because it produces futility (v. 17) and emptiness in one's thinking. *"Gentiles"* or unbelievers try to find something—*anything*—to fill that void, by looking for what will—*even temporarily*—bring comfort, pleasure and satisfaction to their lives. Therefore, sensuality (*or something that stirs the sens*es) leads to the first of many indulges for the unbeliever. And the more immoral and risky the choices and behaviors were, *or are*, the more it titillates and draws them *(and us)* into a vacuous hole. Because believers are not immune to this spiral, we should avoid it like a dieter who avoids spending the day in the best bakery in town. *Don't even come near what tempts!*

Thought to take:
Unfortunately, it's not just the Gentiles of old who ran after futile and empty pursuits in order to fill the void of their hearts. As a believer, I'm tempted every day to run after what feels good in the moment, but ultimately draws me away from complete surrender and reliance on God. It is clear from this reading that I should especially avoid certain seductive and sensual temptations, by not putting myself in compromising situations. Instead, I will fill my hunger for more with more of the Lord's sweet and tasty word, as well as comforting and encouraging moments of prayer.

T2t: Taste and see that the Lord is good!

Help: Pray for God's help to apply your T2t both now and all day long.

Father, there is so much at stake in my life each day. I am faced constantly with choices to run back to the futility of my life before coming in faith to You. But I want to remember the consequences and cost of running after those empty and vain things. I want to remember that my heart grows harder and my mind grows darker with every temptation I give into and sin I commit. So keep me by Your side—reminding me to resist sin in Your power. For I know that I lose much more than I gain when I compromise and give in to temptation. And each time I resist temptation, fill me up with more and more of Your joy, comfort and peace. May I come to realize and proclaim that I have tasted and seen that You are indeed, *not just good, but great!* You are the best indulgence this world has ever seen or known! Thank You for bringing light and sensitivity to my life, so that my life can shine brightly for You! In Jesus' name, amen.

Yield: Surrender yourself to God and His truths—reflecting on and applying your T2t all day long.

29 - CHOOSING THE NEW OVER THE OLD

Week 6, Day 4—Ephesians 4:20-23

Welcome the Lord: Ask Him to reveal His truth to you as you study.

Observe what the Scripture says:

20 - *That, however, is not the way of life you learned*
21 - *when you heard about Christ and were taught in him in accordance with the truth that is in Jesus.*
22 - *You were taught, with regard to your former way of life, to put off your old self, which is being corrupted by its deceitful desires;*
23 - *to be made new in the attitude of your minds;*

Recognize what is noteworthy and true:

In yesterday's reading (vv. 17-19), Paul began to share how a believer should *not* act. But here in today's reading, beginning in verse 20, his teaching offers us the flip side of this equation —how believers *should* act. Paul assumed that these Ephesian believers had been taught about the believer's *"way of life."* He knew this because he had visited and lived in Ephesus for some time to support the church start there. At that time, he became well acquainted with one particular ministry leader, Apollos, who had been mentored by Aquila and Priscilla. Apollos was most likely the one to start and continue to shepherd one or more churches in Ephesus. That's why Paul was so confident that these people had been given good instruction on this *way of life.*

In verse 21, Paul detailed exactly *the way* in which these Ephesian believers were taught. They *heard* about Christ, but also were *"taught in him."* This wording reminds me that Christ is ultimately the One who imparts truth and opens our eyes to what is only spiritually derived through and *in Him.* I want to remember this valuable insight whenever I endeavor to teach God's truths to others. It is not up to me to open their eyes; it is an *"inside job"* of the Holy Spirit.

In verse 22, Paul went further to describe exactly *what* the Ephesian believers were taught. They were taught to *"put off the old self"*—which included the practices and beliefs they held before coming to Christ. The idea of putting off something is like taking off certain clothes that we wear. After all, our clothing choices reflect our preferences, current circumstances, and even our identities. It's like I used to wear clothes that reflected the preferences of a teenager; but as an adult, I make different choices. It's the same with our spiritual attire—it should always be *reflective of Christ.* I also note that the former way of life before coming to Christ is constantly *being corrupted* by current deceitful desires. This means that the *"old self"* is controlled by human and depraved desires. But as believers, we must let Christ reign in our hearts, so that we can resist going back to our former way of living and thinking.

The application of the *"way"* we should live our lives as believers is encapsulated in verse 23—*"to be made new in the attitude of your minds."* As a believer, I allow Christ to not only save my soul, but also to continue to save and transform me into His image one day and choice at a time. Therefore, this *"new attitude"* is constantly renewed each time you and I obey the Spirit (Rom. 12:2, 2 Cor. 5:17).

Thought to take:

This reading encourages me to prayerfully consider whether or not my new way of life—*living based on God's truth and love*—is being more clearly and actively demonstrated than my *old self* and way of life that was based on my human logic and desires. As I seek God's perspective, I'm sure He will reveal to me all sorts of weaknesses and areas of my life where I rely too heavily on myself and others. I can choose to recoil and run from those deficits and ultimately back to my *"old self,"* or I can yield those weaknesses to Him, so that He can put on the *"new self"* that reveals the Spirit's regeneration in my life.

T2t: Keep Jesus' new attitude in place

Help: Pray for God's help to apply your T2t both now and all day long.

Father, I want to give a more serious focus to the way of life that I have been taught through Your word and by the spiritual leaders in my life. Use those truths in conjunction with Your Spirit to empower me to leave my former way of life, so that I can live the transformed and new life You have given me. As I go about my day and temptations come my way, may I keep my focus on Your truths, as well as continuing to yield my situation and heart to Your care. I trust You to guide and empower me for every challenge in my life. May others see the transformation You do in me—*unfolding in ways that bring greater glory to You.* And keep my heart poised to respond to Your continual work of regeneration in each choice and challenge I face. Let that create a new attitude that points to and glorifies Your Son, drawing others to Your salvation. In Jesus' name, amen.

Yield: Surrender yourself to God and His truths—reflecting on and applying your T2t all day long.

30 - THE ROBES OF TRUTH AND GRACE

Week 6, Day 5—Ephesians 4:24-27

Welcome the Lord: Ask Him to reveal His truth to you as you study.

Observe what the Scripture says:

24 - *and to put on the new self, created to be like God in true righteousness and holiness.*

25 - *Therefore each of you must put off falsehood and speak truthfully to your neighbor, for we are all members of one body.*

26 - *"In your anger do not sin": Do not let the sun go down while you are still angry,*

27 - *and do not give the devil a foothold.*

Recognize what is noteworthy and true:

In yesterday's reading (vv. 20-23), Paul talked about the old self and way of life for an unbeliever. While today, starting in verse 24, he explained what the *"new self"* or life should look like for the *believer*. He continued using the same metaphor he began with in verse 22, regarding *putting off the old self*; however, he replaced it with the idea of *putting on the new self*. Paul then essentially said that a Christ-follower's spiritual attire should reflect God's *"true righteousness and holiness."* I'm not so sure that my outward appearance *continually* reflects God's righteousness and holiness, but it must be possible or Paul would not have directed believers to pursue this. After all, what I put on each day certainly impacts the way I feel and think about myself. When I dress in clothes that are attractive and new, I feel more attractive—*might even be more attractive to others*. It works the same way when we *put on the new self*. We feel encouraged and become a better representation of Christ to the world.

In verse 25, Paul explained how we put on the new self. We can't keep the old clothes of our former life on while putting on the new self. We must intentionally put off things like *"falsehood"* by speaking truthfully to our neighbors *(everyone)*. This shift enables us to *put on* our new self. Paul offered another reason why we should put off falsehood and the old self; it's because we, as Christ-followers, are all *"members of one body."* These actions we take to put on the new self not only reflect our new life in Christ, but also *reflect our unity with our fellow-believers*.

In verse 26, Paul detailed a list of things believers should avoid with the first being: *"In your anger do not sin."* I notice that Paul did not say that anger is necessarily sinful, but that it *can be sinful*. Anger is simply an emotion that even Christ felt and demonstrated, *though always in the right ways and times*. We, as humans, rarely if ever deal with our anger in Christ-like ways or know which situations warrant an angry response and which do not. These are the things we need to prayerfully consider in order to know if our anger is righteous or sinful. Paul went on to urge believers to *"not let the sun go down while you are still angry."* The idea here is not a literal rule, but rather a guiding principle. We should be quick to deal with our anger in a gracious and Christ-like way—*not letting it remain day after day*.

The reason why we should deal as quickly as possible with our anger (v. 27) is because anger left unchecked gives the devil a *"foothold."* The Greek translation of this word is to not give the enemy room/opportunity to work in our lives. So anger must be resolved and released as a way to protect our hearts.

Thought to take:

This reading reveals two main ways to put on the new life in Christ—*by putting off deception while putting on truth, as well as putting off anger while letting Christ's peace reign.* Of these two, I tend to let anger get the best of me. I certainly don't want to invite spiritual forces of darkness into my life and relationships. And I realize this process involves the difficult task of being truthful with myself, with God and others. Not dealing directly with my anger only lets it fester and grow—creating an atmosphere that pulls Satan toward me like a moth to flame. So I will focus on resolving anger through examination and prayer processing. Then I will respond in gracious ways to others—seeking reconciliation and peace instead.

T2t: Examine and resolve anger quickly

Help: Pray for God's help to apply your T2t both now and all day long.

Father, as a child of the King, You offer me a new and pure wardrobe that reflects Your truth, peace and holiness. So remind me not to return to the filthy rags that I once wore in my former way of life. Instead, enable me to put on Your robe, so that truthfulness and mercy act as my covering and character in all of my interactions today. Remind me that this not only brings honor to You, but is also something You use to unify me with my brothers and sisters in Christ. For I know that when I join with other believers, strutting out into the world in our Christ-honoring *"clothes,"* we can dazzle every onlooker with *Your* brilliance and wealth—*drawing them to You.* Most of all, use my faith-filled actions today to guard my heart and relationships from the influence of the evil one. Keep me safely adorned with the robes of Your righteousness wherever I go this day! In Christ's name, amen.

Yield: Surrender yourself to God and His truths—reflecting on and applying your T2t all day long.

Week Six Group Discussion Questions

4:11-13—Finding Christ's Fullness

What percentage would you rate yourself on how full of Christ you believe you are right now? Based on this day's emphasis, what are some things you could do to improve your fullness in Christ?

4:14-16—How Spiritually Mature Am I?

What hinders you from speaking the *"truth in love"* to others? What are some ways we can do this boldly and graciously with others?

4:17-19—What Hardens Our Hearts

What is one sensual indulgence that tempts you the most? What do you need to do to protect your heart against this temptation?

4:20-23—Choosing the New Over the Old

What are some truths of Christ that you need to *"put on"* and *"live out"* in your life?

4:24-27—The Robes of Truth and Grace

What is a lie you need to tear down in your life? What is a resentment that you need to yield to Christ?

31 - FOCUS ON THE NEEDS OF OTHERS

Week 7, Day 1—Ephesians 4:28-29

Welcome the Lord: Ask Him to reveal His truth to you as you study.

Observe what the Scripture says:

28 - *Anyone who has been stealing must steal no longer, but must work, doing something useful with their own hands, that they may have something to share with those in need.*

29 - *Do not let any unwholesome talk come out of your mouths, but only what is helpful for building others up according to their needs, that it may benefit those who listen.*

Recognize what is noteworthy and true:

Paul listed another way to put off the old self here in verse 28—*so that the new self can be worn, lived out and seen*—by saying we must *"steal no longer."* This might indicate that the people within the Ephesian congregation were stealing. According to historians, stealing was rampant in Ephesus and elsewhere during this time period. It was most common at the docks and public baths where people would leave their belongings unattended while they bathed. Obviously this offered a prime temptation and opportunity to take someone's belongings. Perhaps poverty provoked many to steal, but as believers, they needed to avoid this sinful vice.

One way to change this bad habit was to work doing something useful with their *"own hands"* (v. 28). If the people were stealing due to poverty, they probably were not educated nor highly skilled, so working with their hands would have been their only option for making a living. Maybe Paul knew that some of these people were unwilling to exert themselves, when in their former life they could have easily relied on stealing to get by. They now needed to leave this life behind and *"put on"* attitudes and behaviors that would bring honor to the Lord. I also note that the main reason Paul urged the Ephesians (and us) to find useful and honest sources of income was not to simply support themselves (or ourselves), but instead to be able to *share with others* who are in need. Our focus as believers needs to always be on giving out of what we've been given by the Lord.

Verse 29 has always been an all-time favorite memory verse of mine and, *even decades later*, is still fresh in my mind. The list here of what to put off continued with the instruction *"not to let any unwholesome talk"* come out of our mouths. Other translations for the term *"unwholesome"* are words like: *"corrupting,"* *"abusive,"* *"dirty,"* etc. But the best Greek translation of this word is *"rotten"* or *"worthless."* I think there are a lot of things that I say that could be categorized as *"worthless,"* but saying something *"rotten"* probably takes this to the level of cursing and using abusive language.

Instead, we are to only speak *"what is helpful for building others up according to their needs."* This indicates that we must *pay attention to the needs* of others around us, otherwise we won't know how to build them up. We must be involved in each other's lives—*spurring one another on in our faith* (Heb. 10:24). I also note that the Greek translation of the word *"benefit"* in this verse includes the idea of *"giving grace"* to those who listen. Therefore, my goal as a Christ-follower is to be gracious—*generous and forgiving*—in every word or statement that I say and let pass through my lips.

Thought to take:
It's easy to let myself off the hook when it comes to the idea of

not stealing, since I avoid this nasty habit. But there are other ways I might steal that would include both Paul's instruction not to steal, as well as to not saying worthless things. For example: sometimes I steal the financial help that God desires for me to give to others in need when I'm stingy; sometimes I steal attention from those who need it more than me; and sometimes I steal other people's joy or self-esteem when I say something unkind or hateful to them. There are a myriad of ways that I might steal what God desires for me to give to others. So I will guard my heart, actions and words—giving graciously to the needs *of others* in my life today.

T2t: Speak and give graciously

Help: Pray for God's help to apply your T2t both now and all day long.

Father, as one of Your children, I am so very blessed in a multitude of ways. I never want to forget the spiritual bounty that You lavish on me in life. Use that to motivate me to work hard, but to also give out of the overflow to others who are in need. Also, guard my heart from stealing attention, stealing joy, or simply stealing opportunities that belong to others. Open my eyes and sharpen my heart to hear and pay attention to what other people's needs are so that I can give in ways that meet their needs. And guard my tongue from saying anything that might bring dishonor to You—*going further to speak words that offer grace in every encounter I have today and every day of my life.* I want my focus to be on giving what builds up other people, just like You build up and bless *my life* each day! In Christ's name, amen.

Yield: Surrender yourself to God and His truths—reflecting on and applying your T2t all day long.

32 - OUR SIN—HIS FORGIVENESS

Week 7, Day 2—Ephesians 4:30-32

Welcome the Lord: Ask Him to reveal His truth to you as you study.

Observe what the Scripture says:
30 - *And do not grieve the Holy Spirit of God, with whom you were sealed for the day of redemption.*
31 - *Get rid of all bitterness, rage and anger, brawling and slander, along with every form of malice.*
32 - *Be kind and compassionate to one another, forgiving each other, just as in Christ God forgave you.*

Recognize what is noteworthy and true:
Paul seemed to pause his teaching on putting off and putting on, in verse 30, to encapsulate what happens when we do not follow through on these important choices. When we choose to *put on* sin, we *"grieve the Holy Spirit."* This tells me at least two things: one, that the Holy Spirit is a personal God with emotions; and two, that believers impact the Spirit for good or for ill by our choices. I know that any of my family's bad choices can cause me to feel grieved, but this is only out of my love and concern for them, and never severs my relationship with them. In the same way, Paul assured us believers are *"sealed for the day of redemption;"* so even though, as a believer, my sin grieves the Spirit, it cannot remove the seal of my redemption secured and

won by Christ.

In verse 31, Paul resumed pointing out the sins that believers are to avoid and *"get rid of"* in our lives. *To get rid of* implies that sins like these listed here have already been committed. Paul wasn't being judgmental here, since he likely witnessed these people speaking in bitter and angry ways. He also must have seen them brawling, or the Greek is better translated *"clamoring,"* which involves some type of wrathful *outcry*. His final observation was that they demonstrated *"every form of malice,"* which is better-translated *wickedness*. If this was what Paul saw and knew was evident in their lives, then as their spiritual leader, he had a responsibility to call them to a new way of living. Otherwise, how will unbelievers ever know how Christ can transform our lives without our lives giving evidence of His Spirit? These types of sins—*related to anger and bitterness*—show much more obviously in our actions, words and choices. They might even cause more damage in all sorts of ways than other kinds of sins; *though, as a believer, all sin should be resisted and, if committed, confessed.*

In verse 32, Paul offered the remedy for putting off these sins when he commanded believers to *"be kind and compassionate."* When I truly operate out of the Spirit's kindness and compassion, my anger begins to dissipate and disappear. When I take the time to see things through other people's eyes—*through Christ's compassion*—I am able to let go of my anger and bitterness. I am then also able to *"forgive"* them. I note that this is not just forgiveness offered for the sake of freeing myself from my anger, but is also my duty and obligation as one who has received forgiveness from Christ for my sin. In my experience, when I've taken on this perspective shift—*focusing on Christ's forgiveness of me*—it has made forgiving others impossible to resist!

Thought to take:

One of the most important thoughts to focus on from this

powerful reading is to avoid holding on to anger and bitterness, as well as all the manifestations that bitterness can produce in my life. Since, as a believer, I am sealed by the Holy Spirit, I need to remember that these kinds of longstanding angry attitudes and choices grieve the Spirit—though they never remove the Spirit from my life. So I will prayerfully pay attention to the condition of my heart and how I'm interacting with others to see if I am holding on to anger. When I am, I will seek the Spirit's power to be kind and compassionate instead. I will do this by reminding myself of how Christ has forgiven me of my sins, so that I can let go of other's sins against me.

T2t: Replace anger with compassion

Help: Pray for God's help to apply your T2t both now and all day long.

Father, what a personal and intimate God You are that even Your Spirit within me is stirred to grief when I disobey You! But I wouldn't expect You to be any other way. Let me never forget that my sin—*no matter how small or significant it seems*—impacts You in profound ways. I never want to make Your Spirit uncomfortable or cause You to recoil from my sinful heart. So make it obvious to me whenever I'm being tempted to act on my anger in ways that are hurtful or even wicked in my relationships. May I then remember what is at stake, *like my testimony of Your transformation in my life!* Help me to resist those temptations and to put on Your kindness and compassion instead—*always remembering the forgiveness I possess through Christ!* When I view myself in relation to others from that perspective, it humbles and compels me to let their offenses go at Christ's nail-scarred feet. Let that be my continual focus and motivation today! In Christ's name, amen.

Yield: Surrender yourself to God and His truths—reflecting on and applying your T2t all day long.

33 - STAYING IN STEP
WITH THE FATHER

Welcome the Lord: Ask Him to reveal His truth to you as you study.

Observe what the Scripture says:

1 - Follow God's example, therefore, as dearly loved children
2 - and walk in the way of love, just as Christ loved us and gave himself up for us as a fragrant offering and sacrifice to God.
3 - But among you there must not be even a hint of sexual immorality, or of any kind of impurity, or of greed, because these are improper for God's holy people.

Recognize what is noteworthy and true:

In some ways, Paul's language up to this point and chapter —*the idea of putting off and putting on*—deals more with outward expressions that reflect an inward change through Christ. But starting off here in verse 1, Paul revealed more the inner motivation and focus for our conduct as believers. Christ-followers are to *"follow God's example"* as *"dearly loved children."* The Father's love for believers, as His dearly loved children, should move us to turn from our sins and back toward Him and His loving relationship with us. In application, this is like being a tot that's trying desperately to keep up with my loving Father so that I can grab His hand and stay in step with Him. Thankfully, *He never leaves me behind!*

In verse 2, Paul gave another prime focus and motivation for the believer by teaching us to *"walk in the way of love, just as Christ loved us."* Therefore, not only do you and I need to stay in step with our loving Father, but we also need to chase after our Savior who—*out of His great love for the world*—showed us the *"way of love."* This means Christ's love provides a *"fragrant offering and sacrifice to God."* There are many examples in the Old Testament when an animal sacrifice served as a pleasing aroma to God (Gen. 8:21; Ex. 29:18, 25, 41; Lev. 19, 13, 17, etc.). This wasn't because of the rapturous smell of steak on the altar, but because it represented the humble repentance of the people bringing the offering. Just think of how much more pleasing Christ's sacrifice for our sins must have been for the Father, even as it also broke His heart to see His Son die for our sins. This indicates that when you and I walk in the way of Christ's love, our sacrifices and offerings to the Lord *smell fragrant* and please Him immensely.

In verse 3, Paul took a decidedly quick turn in a different direction by, once again, providing what *"holy people"* (or some translations say *"saints"—meaning believers*) should *put off and avoid altogether*. Therefore, the *"saint"* should not show *"even a hint of sexual immorality," "impurity,"* nor *"greed."* Sexual immorality seems obvious, but *"impurity"* or *"uncleanness"* was more of a broad term that indicates avoiding anything that corrupts and defiles our character. Like bitterness and malice (4:31), sexual immorality and impurity are obvious deviations from God's self-control and purity. If I am to follow God's example, I will not allow even a hint of this attitude to seep into my mind, nor come out in my actions. Apparently, greed can be just as obvious and corrupting to the believer's testimony and heart as sexual immorality. All such sins are *"improper"* for *saints of God*.

Thought to take:

I see from this reading just how important it is to avoid certain sins like sexual immorality, impurity and greed. I cannot even allow a hint of these pursuits to invade my heart and mind. I cannot justify what I let my eyes linger on, nor indulge in earthly delights that take my eyes off my Lord for even one second. I must remember how corrupting these pursuits are to the heart Christ died to redeem and purify with His blood. If I want to stay in step with the Father—*which I do!*—I must guard my heart's purity by resisting these sins and chasing after Him instead.

T2t: Resist sin and chase after God instead

Help: Pray for God's help to apply your T2t both now and all day long.

Father, help me to chase after You each step of the way in this life. And thank You for reminding me that I am Your dearly loved child. This encourages me to follow Your example and to walk in the way of Christ's love and sacrifice. May my obedient choices, *done through Your Spirit's power*, waft toward heaven in a pleasing aroma that reminds You of Your Son and His fragrant sacrifice on the cross. Protect me from going my own way toward selfish pursuits that gratify my sinful desires. For You know how seductive and insidious sexual immorality, impurity and greed can seem in the moment. *Yet Christ was able to resist these sins every single time He was tempted!* Enable me to do the same—running far from those temptations and fiercely in Your direction as quickly as I can. And use my obedience as an outward demonstration of the life-transformational power of Your love, so that others become convinced that You are my loving Father and Lord! In Jesus' name, amen.

Yield: Surrender yourself to God and His truths—reflecting on and applying your T2t all day long.

34 - OUR WORDS REFLECT
WHO WE ARE

Week 7, Day 4—Ephesians 5:4-5

Welcome the Lord: Ask Him to reveal His truth to you as you study.

Observe what the Scripture says:
4 - *Nor should there be obscenity, foolish talk or coarse joking, which are out of place, but rather thanksgiving.*
5 - *For of this you can be sure: No immoral, impure or greedy person —such a person is an idolater—has any inheritance in the kingdom of Christ and of God.*

Recognize what is noteworthy and true:
The list continues to grow of all the sinful and foolish actions needing to be *put off* (4:22ff) as Christ-followers (v. 4). First off, Paul added *"obscenity"* or several other translations use the word *"filthiness"* to his growing list. The best translation of *"obscenity"* in the Greek is *"baseness."* The idea behind *"baseness"* is that we should avoid scraping the bottom of the moral barrel in any of our conversations and/or actions.

The second action we should avoid—*"foolish talk"*—is reflective of and dovetails with the first action to avoid—*obscenity* (v. 4). The Greek word for foolish talk is *"mōrologia."* Interestingly, this is the only place you can find this word being used in the New Testament. It means we should avoid having meaningless conversations that do not build others up in some way, or even tear others down. Perhaps these pointless conversations, ironically, might point others to idolatrous choices like sexual immorality, since it was mentioned within this context.

The third action Paul instructed believers to put off is *"coarse joking,"* which also was used only this one time here in the New Testament. This terminology involves telling a dirty joke or joking in a way that brings dishonor to Christ or the Gospel. It is undignified and reflects immoral thoughts and standards. There is nothing funny about jokes like these told through the lips of a Christ-follower. This kind of joking, as Paul stated, is *"out of place"* in the Christian community and elsewhere. It is as if we are spitting out excrement or spreading a contagious disease, whenever we share these off-colored jokes.

Paul then gave what believers are to *put on* and practice each day—*the intentional act of giving thanks to our Lord*. I take this to mean that anytime I am tempted to act in these corrupt and immoral ways, I should resist by *giving thanks to the Lord for His many blessings in my life—including the joy of sex in marriage*. When I make that choice, the pull to sin loses its power over my heart and life.

In verse 5, Paul called *a spade a spade*, when he said that anyone who sets about to live an immoral, impure and greedy lifestyle (all things he mentioned in v. 3), he is an *"idolater"* and cannot expect to receive a believer's *"inheritance in the kingdom of Christ and of God."* The term idolater involves a *lifestyle* of these sins. It does not mean that if we commit these acts— *essentially committing idolatry*—we can expect to lose our salvation, though ongoing repentance and resistance is essential. To continue to live an immoral, impure and greedy lifestyle gives evidence that salvation never occurred for that person in the first place. Christ-followers are always grieved and convicted by these types of sins and return in repentance at some, not-too-distant point in their lives.

Thought to take:

I'm not one to tell dirty jokes or talk in obscene ways, but some of the things I've said in my life surely fall under the category of *"foolish talk."* I'm reminded and convicted today about the need to filter everything that I say through the grid of whether it *builds others up or not.* I also see what is at stake when I allow these kinds of sins to creep into my conversations and flow out in my actions. They bring dishonor to the Lord and muddy the pure waters of the confession I make as a Christ-follower. Therefore, if it is worthless or, *worse, corrupting,* then I should take that thought and word captive—choosing instead to thank God for His blessings in this life.

T2t: Let my words and life reflect Christ

Help: Pray for God's help to apply your T2t both now and all day long.

Father, there are so many things that I say in any given day that I do not always take seriously. But I'm reminded today of the need to guard my mind and lips in every thought and conversation I might have in life. My choices matter and are not neutral or to be overlooked simply because people find them funny or entertaining. I must remember to always take any impure thoughts and words captive to Your pure Spirit—*yielding my will and way to Yours. Please, help me in this quest!* I also pray that my life would reflect Your goodness and purity—pointing others to Christ as a result. May my choices be awe-inspiring and winsome to believers and unbelievers alike. Empower me to live a lifestyle that brings honor to You in all I do and say each day. In Jesus' name, amen.

Yield: Surrender yourself to God and His truths—reflecting on and applying your T2t all day long.

35 - WHICH SIDE ARE YOU ON?

Week 7, Day 5—Ephesians 5:6-8

Welcome the Lord: Ask Him to reveal His truth to you as you study.

Observe what the Scripture says:

6 - *Let no one deceive you with empty words, for because of such things God's wrath comes on those who are disobedient.*
7 - *Therefore do not be partners with them.*
8 - *For you were once darkness, but now you are light in the Lord. Live as children of light*

Recognize what is noteworthy and true:

Paul began verse 6 by urging these believers and us to *"let no one deceive you with empty words."* This could've been a general principle and idea, but it could have also been that Paul was specifically pointing out a particular group to avoid. Naturally, this could have simply referred to the old and unsaved friends and family of these new believers, who were probably unhappy with their friends' decisions to follow Christ. This choice and change of lifestyle surely felt fanatical and prudish to unbelievers. They might have used *empty* and hollow promises of sex, money and thrills to bait their believing friends to come back to their former disobedient lifestyles. But Paul wanted them to remember that God's wrath comes against those who live disobediently. Cheap thrills would soon and always do lead to destruction.

I would be remiss to leave out another group whose false teachings were prevalent at this time in history—*the Gnostics*. Gnostics believed and taught that the spirit was the only holy and good aspect within a person and that the body or any type of *"matter"* was evil and unimportant. Since the body was evil, it was to be despised—*giving focus and attention only to the spirit within a person*. Gnostics justified that partaking in every form of sin and immorality was fine, because the body or *"matter" did not matter*. Ironically, nothing could be further from the truth according to the Gospel.

In verse 7, the term *"partner"* is used in the NIV, while many other translations use the term *"partaker"* instead. But the Greek implies not just partaking alone and for one time, but a co-partaking or partnership in sin. Therefore, *"partner"* provides a more detailed and clear picture of the danger of participating with old friends' sins. This partnership in sin, at the very least, casts a dishonoring shadow on the message of Christ, if not leading others—*including ourselves*—astray.

Picture, if you will, a light being turned off just as Paul spoke these words to the Ephesians in verse 8, *"For you were once darkness."* We all know what it's like to be engulfed in darkness. We do not know where to walk or what perils lie in our path. But then let's say, Paul turns the lights on when he said *"but now you are light in the Lord."* We can see again. We know where to walk and what to avoid because the Spirit illuminates our hearts and minds. In fact, believers must *"live as children of light"*—reflecting Christ's light that inspires, brightens and warms those in the world. We also must shine a light on sin in our and other people's lives. Therefore, we live as *inspiring*, as well as *frighteningly convicting* lights in the world.

Thought to take:

I want to remember and recognize that every choice I make to sin is not neutral, nor remains free from entanglements or partnerships in sin. It's like knowing that I'm on one team, while deciding to make a goal or touchdown for the opposing team. I could argue, *"It's just one touchdown!"* But everyone would see the destructiveness, as well as *insanity* of my singular choice in that moment. So I will commit to remain true to my team, my spiritual family and Christ's headship by shining as a light for Christ alone.

T2t: Let my choices shine for Christ

Help: Pray for God's help to apply your T2t both now and all day long.

Father, keep me focused on You and Your leadership in my life today and everyday. Help me to never listen to the empty promises this world tries to whisper in my ear; but rather keep me attuned to Your voice and leading in all things. For I know that Your way brings me the fulfillment and joy I long for in this life. My life before You was shrouded in darkness and confusion. I did not know how or where to walk until Your Spirit lit me up from the inside out. May I find ways to stoke the flames of Your Spirit by avoiding sin and living in the light of Your word and the power of Your Son. Open the eyes of those who are in my life to Your life-transforming power shown through my obedience to You. And use Your light in me to reveal to them how empty and futile life is without You. Enable them to abandon those dark and vain pursuits in favor of Your shining grace and glory. In Jesus' name, amen.

Yield: Surrender yourself to God and His truths—reflecting on and applying your T2t all day long.

Week Seven Group Discussion Questions

4:28-29—Focus on the Needs of Others

In what ways might you be stealing what rightfully belongs to others? *(Think outside the box here!)* How can you improve on the things you say and do to benefit those you interact with?

4:30-32—Our Sin—His Forgiveness

Which of these hate-filled sins are you tempted to cling to in life, and why? What are some ways you can respond with kindness, compassion and forgiveness to those you who hurt and offend you?

5:1-3—Staying in Step with the Father

What positive impact would showing Christ's love to others do for them? What situations have tempted you most to indulge impure or greedy thoughts? What has God redeemed and turned around for good in your life?

5:4-5—Our Words Reflect Who We Are

What are some things or people you might be making an idol in your life? How can you protect yourself against these temptations?

5:6-8—Which Side Are You On?

When have you been influenced by others to return to a particular sin? What is one thing you want to do in order to more effectively reflect Christ's light to others?

36 - HEALING AND REVEALING LIGHT

Week 8, Day 1—*Ephesians 5:9-13*

Welcome the Lord: Ask Him to reveal His truth to you as you study.

Observe what the Scripture says:
9 - (for the fruit of the light consists in all goodness, righteousness and truth)
10 - And find out what pleases the Lord.
11 - Have nothing to do with the fruitless deeds of darkness, but rather expose them.
12 - It is shameful even to mention what the disobedient do in secret.
13 - But everything exposed by the light becomes visible—and everything that is illuminated becomes a light.

Recognize what is noteworthy and true:
The mention of the *"fruit of the light,"* in verse 9, is a metaphor related to how the sun helps to produce fruit on trees, bushes and vines. For in the same way, God's light, or some translations say *"Spirit,"* produces *fruit* in our lives like *"goodness, righteousness and truth"* (see Gal. 5:22-23 for more *"fruit"*). The Greek word for *"goodness"* is agathōsunē and means we should have a generosity of spirit. The Greek word for *"righteousness"* is dikaiosunē and involves a just mindset that gives to others what they are due. The Greek word here for *"truth"* is alētheia and involves not just knowing, but *living out* moral truths as well.

Paul continued this same thought (v. 10) by summing up what the aim should be for *"children of the light"* (v. 8). We should *"find out"* what pleases the Lord. The Greek translation of *"find out"* involves *testing* something in order to live out what is approved by God. The Spirit and light of God helps us to discern what are God's will and truths so that we can live lives that are approved by Him.

Paul's words again (v. 11) urge believers to *"have nothing to do with the fruitless deeds of darkness,"* which points back to his reference to darkness in 5:8. Every believer has been called out of darkness and into the Lord's light through Christ's salvation. If we remain in the dark in a spiritual sense, we cannot grow nor produce the fruit of the Spirit. Our call is to come out of the dark and into the light of God's truth—*allowing the Spirit to expose not just other people's sins with God's light, but also our own sins.* In fact, this should be the place we *start first*—focusing on our own hearts (Mt. 7:5).

In verse 12, Paul knew that to expose sin with God's light might tempt believers to talk and focus too much on sins, and not enough on God's light and truth. We shouldn't spend our days discussing all the ways that a particular *"shameful"* sin captured and deceived us or others, when we could be focusing on God's truth and reveling in His light instead. We are to take those sins captive (2 Cor. 10:5).

Paul reminds us again, in verse 13, of the impact of God's light on our lives. It *"exposes"* not just a portion, but also *"everything"*—making all that is hidden or in darkness *visible*. There is something unnerving and even alarming when a bright light shines on us after sleeping in the dark. But once we are awake and see the beauty, warmth and healing power of the light of Christ, we are drawn toward the light—*toward Him*—and throw wide open our curtains so that Christ's light beams down on all!

Thought to take:
This reading reveals two contrasts—doing what pleases the

Lord, and avoiding what doesn't. The only way I can strike this tension is to rely on God's light to shine brightly in my life. So I will set about to learn His word, pray and apply His truths in my life—letting God expose any sins I'm harboring with *His light*. This also involves avoiding *the dark* by not getting caught up in fruitless conversations or ruminations about my or other's past or current failures. Instead, I will look to God's light to empower me to be generous, just and moral in all I do, think and say today and each day moving forward.

T2t: Be generous, just and moral

Help: Pray for God's help to apply your T2t both now and all day long.

Father, I am challenged today to consider whether I'm consistently producing the fruit of Your light in my life. Reveal to me the answers to these questions: *How often do I give generously and sacrificially of my resources to others on any given day? How much do I focus on giving others what they are due, rather than focusing on what is due me? And to what degree am I living out Your truths?* Are these spiritual fruits evident and obvious to all I relate with and know? Help me to grow in all of these areas as I set about to study, pray and apply Your truths and light to my life. Keep me from worthless conversations about any shameful sins I, or any others, have committed. Enable me to focus daily on the healing and revealing power of Your light and truth—*never recoiling from Your light, but rather running toward it and basking in it all the days of my life!* In Jesus' name, amen.

Yield: Surrender yourself to God and His truths—reflecting on and applying your T2t all day long.

37 - WAKE UP AND BE WISE

Week 8, Day 2—Ephesians 5:14-17

Welcome the Lord: Ask Him to reveal His truth to you as you study.

Observe what the Scripture says:

14 - *This is why it is said: "Wake up, sleeper, rise from the dead, and Christ will shine on you."*
15 - *Be very careful, then how you live—not as unwise but as wise,*
16 - *making the most of every opportunity, because the days are evil.*
17 - *Therefore do not be foolish, but understand what the Lord's will is.*

Recognize what is noteworthy and true:

Paul began verse 14 by quoting lines from what was probably a familiar Christian chorus of the early church, with some scholars speculating that it might've been sung at baptisms during this time period. These lyrics—*"Wake up, sleeper, rise from the dead, and Christ will shine on you"*—flow perfectly from yesterday's reading (vv. 9-13), where Paul urged believers to let the light of Christ expose what is in darkness.

It sounds to me as if Paul was speaking both about *believers and unbelievers* here. As believers, we can easily be lulled into a spiritual sleep whenever we run after what the world provides, instead of looking to Christ. The Spirit becomes grieved by our wayward actions and attitudes so that we become dulled to God's voice, just like the person who falls into a deep sleep is unaware of those talking around him. However, unbelievers are not simply asleep. They must *rise from the dead* in a spiritual sense—letting *Christ shine* on them. Both the believer and unbeliever need Christ's light to awaken them from spiritual sleep or death. Also, it is not up to you or me to wake up to Christ, *but Christ's Light shines and jostles us* out of our slumber. I need to cooperate with the Spirit, instead of hitting my *snooze button*, where I continue to sin and remain unmoved by the Spirit's conviction.

Verse 15 is a generalized call to action, much like verse 10. Only this time we are to *"be careful"* and live in God's wisdom, rather than being unwise or foolish like those who live in darkness. This involves a more specific rallying call—*"making the most of every opportunity, because the days are evil"* (v. 16). Paul was emphasizing how there are specific opportunities given to every believer each day. This reminds me of his words in verse 10—*declaring that God determined and prepared certain good works to be done by us in our lifetimes before we were ever born.* Therefore, I must be on the lookout for these opportunities and be *"wise"* about how I approach them—*giving my all in every opportunity.* And if all of this were not enough reason to be wise, Paul provided yet another motivator—because *"the days are evil."* If the days were evil back then, then how much more corrupt and evil are they today? Therefore, as a child of the light, I have a duty and privilege to shine Christ's light in order to push back darkness in every corner of my life and world.

Paul reemphasized in verse 16 this idea of choosing wisdom over foolishness. The plain and simple truth of how to avoid foolishness in our walk with the Lord is by coming to understand what the Lord's will is. I cannot understand it *on my own*, but I can when I rely on and turn to the Spirit's illumination within me to understand God's truths and will.

Thought to take:
Even though I might be very much awake in spiritual terms, this reading reminds me of how easy it is to be lulled into spiritual

laziness and slumber in life. And the way to avoid this slide toward spiritual sleepiness is to grow in spiritual wisdom—taking every opportunity God gives me to do His will and apply His truths. So I will turn to God's word to find illumination about His truths and will for every situation and problem I face. Then I will press God's truth further into my heart through prayer, application and yielding to His wisdom at every turn in my day.

T2t: Seek and apply God's wisdom

Help: Pray for God's help to apply your T2t both now and all day long.

Father, open my eyes with Your light. Expose every bit of laziness and apathy I might have in my relationship with You and those You call me to love. For I want my faith to be vibrant, energetic and reflective of the light of Christ's resurrection power. Help others to be drawn to the Savior's light and might through my awakened soul. And strengthen my ability to know Your will each day—going on to illuminate my understanding of Your truths each time I read and study Your word. Empower me to then live Your truths out in all that I think, do and say. Use the wisdom that You impart to me to richly encourage all who I encounter this day and every day. In Jesus' name, amen.

Yield: Surrender yourself to God and His truths—reflecting on and applying your T2t all day long.

38 - IS THE 'COMFORTER' COMFORTABLE?

Week 8, Day 3—Ephesians 5:18-20

Welcome the Lord: Ask Him to reveal His truth to you as you study.

Observe what the Scripture says:
18 - *Do not get drunk on wine, which leads to debauchery. Instead, be filled with the Spirit,*
19 - *speaking to one another with psalms, hymns, and songs from the Spirit. Sing and make music from your heart to the Lord,*
20 - *always giving thanks to God the Father for everything, in the name of our Lord Jesus Christ.*

Recognize what is noteworthy and true:
Paul continued here, in verse 18, to identify one very *foolish* choice (refer to v. 17) that believers should avoid—to *"get drunk on wine."* Paul's concern here might have been to warn the new Gentile believers against continuing to join in on the feasts of *"Bacchus."* Bacchus was the pagan *"god of wine"* that people celebrated in that day by indulging in drunkenness, orgies and reckless revelry.

Of course, Paul was not condemning all drinking here, but condemned drinking alcohol to the point of drunkenness, which *"leads to debauchery."* Other translations say it leads to *"excess," "reckless living"* or *"ruin."* The Greek translation of this idea is that our lives can become wasteful or even beyond saving. This doesn't mean that getting drunk as a believer results in losing your salvation. But it must indicate that we waste and lose many God-given opportunities (v. 16) to live out our faith in any meaningful and God-honoring way, whenever we drink to excess.

Paul offered the remedy and refocus of the believer's life by urging us to be filled with the Spirit instead. If I am drunk, I lose self-control and grieve the Holy Spirit's power, as well as drowning out His inner voice. It's important to clarify that when we receive Christ's salvation, His Spirit comes to indwell our hearts—*never leaving us*. But our hearts can become cluttered with so many things that crowd out the *"filling"* of the Spirit. So we must continually seek the Spirit's filling as we go along in our faith walk. The idea of *being filled* is stated in the Greek passive—*meaning something we cannot manufacture on our own*—and in the imperative—*meaning it is something essential to our faith.*

In verse 19, Paul shared how we can specifically fill up our hearts by identifying an important spiritual practice: *"speaking to one another with psalms, hymns, and songs from the Spirit."* When we *"sing and make music"* from our hearts to the Lord, it must invite the Spirit to fill up every part of our heart. Another way God uses our worship is to drown out sinful thoughts, urges and self-centered focuses—realigning our focus on Him. Choices like these are what *please* God (5:10).

Another practice that stirs up the Spirit within us is found in verse 20, when Paul mentioned giving *"thanks to God the Father for everything..."* This indicates prayer, since it is thanks given *"in the name of our Lord Jesus Christ."* I also see that we are to thank God *in prayer* for *"everything."* This tells me that I must remember that the Lord is weaving His best in my life—*redeeming the bad and loss-filled moments that I experience in a fallen world alongside other sinful human beings*—and is replacing them with His good. I don't have to thank Him for the bad, but I should thank Him for how He is using it to bring about His undaunted will that I may not fully see until eternity.

Thought to take:

Paul offers yet again a contrast between what to avoid and what to embrace. In order to strike this tension I must avoid anything, like drunkenness, that distracts and drowns out the Spirit's filling and complete control of my life. I also need to embrace and pursue the Spirit—inviting Him to fill up every part of my heart. There are many things listed in today's reading that provide that welcoming environment. So I will focus on speaking truths of encouragement to other believers, singing songs of worship, and thanking God in *"everything"* all throughout this day and beyond.

T2t: Avoid what distracts and pursue what attracts God

Help: Pray for God's help to apply your T2t both now and all day long.

Father, I realize just how easily my heart can grow cluttered —making Your Spirit uncomfortable, even though You never leave me, nor forsake me. So open my eyes to any sinful distractions or lingering sins that I am ignoring or not yielding to You. Then give me the resolve to turn them over—*one-by-one*—so that my heart is filled up with more of Your Spirit and less of me and my sin. Remind me to engage in spiritual practices and pursuits that encourage Your Spirit's filling. And I promise to speak Your truths to others so that they too can be encouraged to follow You and Your light. I also commit to singing songs that Your Spirit loves to hear, as well as offering You thanks for all You are doing in my life. I trust Your redemption not just of my heart, but also of every part of my life. In Jesus' name, amen.

Yield: Surrender yourself to God and His truths—reflecting on and applying your T2t all day long.

39 - MOTIVE FOR SUBMISSION

Week 8, Day 4—Ephesians 5:21-24

Welcome the Lord: Ask Him to reveal His truth to you as you study.

Observe what the Scripture says:

21 - *Submit to one another out of reverence for Christ.*
22 - *Wives, submit yourselves to your own husbands as you do to the Lord.*
23 - *For the husband is the head of the wife as Christ is the head of the church, his body, of which he is the Savior.*
24 - *Now as the church submits to Christ, so also wives should submit to their husbands in everything.*

Recognize what is noteworthy and true:

Paul's thoughts on submission, in verse 21, relate to all that he shared up to this point regarding living wisely and as lights in the world for Christ, since submission is yet another way to honor Christ. The word Paul used for *"submit"* is a military term that literally means, *"to be under rank."* This means that as a *general* rule *(pardon the pun!)*, we should practice a team or *"troop"* mentality by submitting to other believers whenever possible. We do this *"out of reverence for Christ"*—ultimately submitting to *Him as our Commander in Chief over all.*

In verse 22, Paul narrowed his focus to the Christian wife's need to submit to her husband. Again, this is the same military term used in verse 21. And the reason for this is not because wives are considered less intelligent or less valuable than their husbands, nor is it because it's the *"polite"* thing to do necessarily. Christian wives are to submit to their husbands as they *"do to the Lord."* Christ is our motivation for being submissive in marriage. It is reflective of our submission to Him above all.

Verse 23 continues to focus on this rank established in marriage, even as *all* believers must submit to one another as often as possible. The husband is the *"head"* and given authority over his wife and family, just like Christ is the head of the church— *His bride*—since He gave His life to *save* her. This might seem like a harsh and negative reality for believing wives to swallow, *but the husband is charged with the harder and weightier responsibility here.* Believing husbands must answer to the Lord for every choice their families make, as well as being willing to *give their lives* for the betterment and protection of their wives and families. When a husband operates with this mindset and behavior, his wife should want to submit. But when he doesn't operate this way, and aside from abuses, the wife should still submit to her husband as unto the Lord—*demonstrating her submission to Christ.*

Paul further emphasized the way this should all work and look in verse 24. Just as believers submit to Christ, believing wives should submit to their husbands in *"everything."* Again, this is assuming the husband is *not abusing* his wife. There are other examples in the Bible of disobedient authorities *abusing power* such as: Exodus 1:16-17, Daniel 3:16-18, 6:7-10, Acts 4:19, that give us more insight into this complex issue. Therefore, *"in everything"* involves submitting when a husband is leading, even when those ways feel unfair or foolish to the wife, *yet are not abusive.*

Thought to take:

This reading makes it clear that submission should be a godly attribute and pursuit of *every* believer. But as a believing wife, I am specifically directed here to submit to *my husband*, just like I should submit to the Lord out of my love and trust in Him. So I will focus on submitting to my husband as an act that reflects my reverence for and trust of Christ. For those who are husbands, the most obvious takeaway is to be sacrificial like our Savior—*loving your wife like Christ loves His bride, the church*.

T2t: Submit to Christ out of love and trust

Help: Pray for God's help to apply your T2t both now and all day long.

Dear Jesus, submission always seems to be such a difficult issue for me, but it really shouldn't be when I consider Your example. You were and are so humble and submissive to Your Father because of Your love for Him and trust in Him. I realize that if I want to reflect Your attitude and follow in Your example, I also need to submit to other believers out of reverence for You. I'm grateful You have created and designed this same order in marriage, so that we can reflect the humble way that the church should submit to You our Savior. After all, You lovingly gave Your life to save us from the penalty of death and separation from You that our sins demanded! So being submissive to my spouse *as unto You* is really the least I can do for You, my Savior! I pray that this humble yielding that I commit to practice in my marriage will bring honor to You and demonstrate my trust in Your redemptive and constant care of my life. In Your name, amen.

Yield: Surrender yourself to God and His truths—reflecting on and applying your T2t all day long.

40 - THE HIGH CALLING TO LOVE

Week 8, Day 5—Ephesians 5:25-27

Welcome the Lord: Ask Him to reveal His truth to you as you study.

Observe what the Scripture says:
25 - *Husbands, love your wives, just as Christ loved the church and gave himself up for her*
26 - *to make her holy, cleansing her by the washing with water through the word,*
27 - *and to present her to himself as a radiant church, without stain or wrinkle or any other blemish, but holy and blameless.*

Recognize what is noteworthy and true:
Paul moved his focus from wives submitting to their husbands, in the previous passage, to a higher calling for husbands to love their wives here in verse 25. I would say that submitting to my mate does not require *love* necessarily, but rather trust in the Lord. But for the husband to love his wife, he must be deeply sacrificial and committed, as well as respectful and deferential. He is called to the harder task; *though, for a marriage to thrive, the wife must choose to love her husband each day as well.*

The motivation for the believing husband should be to love his wife because Christ *"loved the church and gave Himself up for her"* (v. 25). If a believing husband wants to truly follow in Christ's footsteps, this is his calling, task and path. And the love God calls the husband to should not be dependent on how lovable his wife acts, since Christ loved the world, even as the world sinned and rejected Him (Rom. 5:8). The Greek word used here for *"love"* is God's completely sacrificial and unconditional love—*"agape."* This is in contrast to a husband relying on *"eros"*—the Greek word for attraction-based love.

Another motivator is given in verse 26 for a believing husband to love his wife—*"to make her holy, cleansing her by the washing with water through the word,"* just like Christ does for the church. This means that God uses the love of believing husbands to actually stimulate and produce more holiness and spiritual cleansing of their wives' hearts. The phrase regarding washing with water through the *"word"* is rather confusing. *Sorry, fellas, but this isn't about the husband giving his wife a bath!* The key to understanding what Paul meant here is in the Greek word used for *"word"* (v. 25), which is *"rhema."* This involves *speaking God's word* and indicates that the believing husband should regularly discuss God's word with his wife, as well as teaching her biblical truths from his own studies. Actually, this process where husband and wife stay in, study God's word and discuss it will wash the hearts of both spouses—knitting their clean hearts as one in the Lord. *It's a total win-win!*

Verse 27 reveals that this process results in something miraculous, like Christ's redemption of the church. Through Christ's cleansing of His bride, she can be presented to Him as His *"radiant church, without stain or wrinkle or any other blemish, but holy and blameless."* Apparently, when a husband loves and nurtures his wife in the spiritual ways mentioned in verses 25-26, she becomes *"radiant"* and is made perfect and *"holy,"* as well. This allows the light of Christ to shine more brightly through the wife's devotion to Jesus. This godly and holy life is greatly supported and ushered in as the husband fulfills his calling and duty to and for his wife.

Thought to take:

Even though I am not a man, nor a husband, I can and should take this encouragement from Paul to heart as well. Loving my husband like God loves me and with the love God extends to me, can strengthen the bond in my marriage, as well as deepen my faith in the Lord. I also see that one of the ways my husband and I can grow deeper in our faith is to discuss God's truths with each other as often as possible. So today and each day I will choose to love my spouse in deeply committed and sacrificial ways, rather than relying on the fickle emotions of *eros love.* I will also encourage him in his faith by pursuing spiritual and Christ-honoring conversations with him.

T2t: Love my mate while strengthening our faith

Help: Pray for God's help to apply your T2t both now and all day long.

Father, I see that the calling of every believer—*husband or wife*—is to follow in Christ's sacrificial and loving footsteps. I must do this remembering that Christ climbed up the hill of Calvary with a rugged and splintered cross on His back, out of His great and incomprehensible love for the bride He sought to redeem. So empower me with that same dogged and unrelenting determination to love my mate and others, like You love me. May I love when love requires more than I think humanly possible—loving out of the *agape love* You extend to and through me. Shine through my life in radiant ways as I fully devote myself to You, so that others are continually drawn to the light and brilliance of Christ's love. In Jesus' name, amen.

Yield: Surrender yourself to God and His truths—reflecting on and applying your T2t all day long.

Week Eight Group Discussion Questions

5:9-13—Healing and Revealing Light

What is one *"good fruit"* that you really hope God is producing in your life, and why? What are some of the *"fruitless deeds of darkness"* that you hope to avoid? What are some ways you can strengthen your resistance to them?

5:14-17—Wake Up and Be Wise

What types of sins typically lull people into spiritual apathy and slumber? What truths and wise principles from God's word can shed light on how to respond to these temptations?

5:18-20—Is the 'Comforter' Comfortable?

What are some actions you want to take to spiritually encourage yourself and other believers? What past negative situation has God redeemed and turned around for good in your life?

5:21-24—Motive for Submission

When you struggle to submit to others *(in particular with your spouse, if married)—aside from abuses—*what might help you to better follow through?

5:25-27—The High Calling to Love

What is one specific way you can show love to your spouse today *(or others, if you're single)*? What are some biblical truths you would like to discuss with others?

41 - A 'ONE BODY' KIND OF LOVE

Week 9, Day 1—Ephesians 5:28-30

Welcome the Lord: Ask Him to reveal His truth to you as you study.

Observe what the Scripture says:

28 - *In this same way, husbands ought to love their wives as their own bodies. He who loves his wife loves himself.*
29 - *After all, no one ever hated their own body, but they feed and care for their body, just as Christ does the church—*
30 - *for we are members of his body.*

Recognize what is noteworthy and true:

It's important to remember that Paul's instructions to believing husbands were/are much more detailed and demanding than what he gave to wives. After all, he only devoted three verses with minimal instruction to wives, while providing instructions that were twice as long to the believing husbands. *Husbands have a high calling to follow and lofty standard to keep!*

In verse 28, Paul continued to detail what a believing husband's love should look like for his wife. It should be at least as much as he loves his own body. To me, this thought loosely correlates with verse 25, because the husband is called to love his wife to the degree that Christ loved the church when He gave His life for her. I say *"loosely"* because Christ's love for the church rises higher than loving your spouse as much as you love yourself. But certainly the call here for a husband is to put his wife's needs as at least equal to his and, *when the occasion calls for it, above his own.* I think Paul gave this example because loving our own bodies and lives is as natural as breathing. Furthermore, the way this is stated in the Greek lends greater understanding and emphasis to all that Paul was saying here. Paul was essentially urging husbands to love their wives because their wives *"are"* their own bodies, which reflects the oneness God gives to us through the bond of marriage. Paul also inserted a significant paradigm when he said, *"He who loves his wife loves himself."* Paul wanted husbands to know that when they choose to love their wives, it is as if they are actually loving themselves, which ultimately benefits both husband and wife.

This idea is further reinforced in verse 29, with the example of how humans care for their bodies. Paul assumed that *"no one ever hated their own body."* It is *normal* to love our bodies, but abnormal when a person hates his or her own body. Whenever we get hungry, most everyone feeds themselves. And we care for our bodies in all the other ways that are needed as well. So a believing husband should always be aware of and alert to the needs of his wife—making sure that they are met as soon as possible and in the best possible way.

Verse 30 wraps this thought up in the bond of marriage, as well as in the bond of *Christ's body.* We all should bear in mind that how we treat our spouses reflects how we are treating *Christ's body.* This is particularly true for husbands, since their love for their wives reflects their love for Christ and Christ's body.

Thought to take:
In this reading, I see a calling for every husband to love his wife like he loves his own body. But I believe this calling is true and necessary for every believing wife as well. So I will make intentional choices to reflect the same oneness I possess with Christ to and for my spouse. I will also strive to live out Christ's sacrificial love in my marriage as I go about this day. I will do this first

by prayerfully reflecting on how I can love my spouse with the nurture and care I give my own body—living out what I sense God is leading me to do in challenging moments today. And I will also pray for my mate to be able to love me in that same Christ-honoring way.

T2t: Love spouse like I love myself

Help: Pray for God's help to apply your T2t both now and all day long.

(If you're a husband, swap the personal pronouns here to customize this prayer for yourself.)

Father, I am so grateful for the way You use my marriage as a reflection of the love and sacrifice Christ demonstrated when He gave His life for the church. So attune my husband's heart and mind to see my needs—moving him to be compassionate and loving to me like he loves his own body. I pray his love would inspire me to love him sacrificially in return, just like the church rises to love, honor and worship You. Help us both to shed our selfish agendas and to care for one another especially when it is difficult and costly. Use that to draw a watching world to Your glorious and mysterious salvation. I also pray that You would remind us of our oneness through the sacred bond of marriage, as well as our membership in the body of Christ. What a privilege to hold the hand of my husband while on earth—knowing he is also my brother in the kingdom of God. In Jesus' name, amen.

Yield: Surrender yourself to God and His truths—reflecting on and applying your T2t all day long.

42 - ONE PLUS ONE IS ONE

Week 9, Day 2—*Ephesians 5:31-33*

Welcome the Lord: Ask Him to reveal His truth to you as you study.

Observe what the Scripture says:

31 - *"For this reason a man will leave his father and mother and be united to his wife, and the two will become one flesh."*
32 - *This is a profound mystery—but I am talking about Christ and the church.*
33 - *However, each one of you also must love his wife as he loves himself,*

Recognize what is noteworthy and true:

Verse 31 flows from the previous day's text—continuing the thought on how a husband and wife are *"one"* in the Lord, as well as in marriage. Paul quoted from Genesis 2:24, *"For this reason a man will leave his father and mother and be united to his wife, and the two will become one flesh."* These words were originally spoken just after God presented Eve to Adam in the Garden of Eden. Ironically, Adam and Eve did not have a mother or father, so Adam was likely not the one who said this, unless it was under the inspiration of God. But these two would go on to be the first parents who taught this break from the family of origin to their children, in order for a complete union to be formed in marriage. A young couple cannot continue to rely on their parents in financial or emotional ways and truly leave and cleave to each other. Their loyalties will be divided, if they do.

Like most, if not all spiritual truths, God desires for us to demonstrate them in visible and tangible ways for others to see and be inspired by. Verse 32 reveals the most important spiritual truth and *"profound mystery"* behind God's design for marriage. A believer's marriage illustrates the marriage between Christ and the church that Christ died to redeem. Christ would never divorce Himself from the church that He loves and died to save. Therefore, every believer should desire to model this lifelong devotion to his/her mate, as far as it is possible (Romans 12:18). We cannot control what our spouses do, but we have a responsibility and calling by Christ to mirror His love and sacrificial devotion to the church in our marriages each day that we live. When this is impossible, we must make every effort to seek godly counsel and interventions before considering divorce.

In verse 33, Paul wrapped up his teachings on marriage by, once again, reminding every husband to love his wife and every wife to respect her husband. The goal for the believing husband is to reflect Christ's *love*, not just for the sake of his marriage *but, more importantly, for the sake of Christ.* The goal for the believing wife is to demonstrate respect, just like the church should respect, honor, and bring glory to Christ. When we each focus on our own responsibilities in marriage, we fulfill our calling as believers, as well as enriching our marriages. This doesn't mean our spouses will follow suit, but it enhances our influence on them to do the same. And when our spouses do not follow suit, our godly choices will reflect the love of Christ under severe persecution and pain. That must be our aim and focus—*not focusing on ourselves necessarily, and definitely not on how our mate's might be failing us.*

Thought to take:

Paul unveiled the great mystery and importance of fulfilling a believing spouse's role and calling in marriage in this reading. As a wife, my part of this equation—*which is one plus one is one*—is to demonstrate respect for my husband. For the husband, it is to live out the sacrificial love of Christ for his wife. When we do this, we are able to reflect the oneness that is so necessary to our testimony as believers, and results in a greater bond in our marriage as well. Therefore, whenever I'm tempted to go my own way today or to think that my husband is making a wrong decision, I will still show respect to him by remaining one with him, unless abuse is involved. And whenever this feels painful or unfair, I will remember that my choice to respect him ultimately honors Christ and mirrors a godly reflection of Christ's marriage to *His* bride, the church.

T2t: Live out oneness in marriage

Help: Pray for God's help to apply your T2t both now and all day long.

Dear Jesus, there are so many ways that my loyalty to my spouse can be divided. I don't always know what these distractions are or when they are coming my way. So open my eyes to every hurtful and divisive alliance in my life. Give me the motivation and ability to release each one to You so that I can be more devoted and united in marriage. May others see Your mysterious love shown through the love and respect my spouse and I demonstrate to each other and to You, *especially when love is hard and costly*. For I know that is when Your paradoxical love shines most brightly to a world that loves only those who love in return. Know that I will love like You love today, as an expression and offering of my love *for* You, my Bridegroom and Lord. In Your name, amen.

Yield: Surrender yourself to God and His truths—reflecting on and applying your T2t all day long.

43 - A FAMILY THAT HONORS GOD

Week 9, Day 3—Ephesians 6:1-4

Welcome the Lord: Ask Him to reveal His truth to you as you study.

Observe what the Scripture says:
1 - *Children, obey your parents in the Lord, for this is right.*
2 - *"Honor your father and mother"—which is the first commandment with a promise—*
3 - *"so that it may go well with you and that you may enjoy long life on the earth."*
4 - *Fathers, do not exasperate your children; instead, bring them up in the training and instruction of the Lord.*

Recognize what is noteworthy and true:
This is only one of two times that the Apostle Paul directed his thoughts to children—doing so here, as well as in Colossians 3:20. His message beginning here, in verse 1, is plain and simple. Children are *"to obey"* their parents, but the key to how they do this is *"in the Lord."* Having the Lord as their ultimate focus helps provide the motivation for following through when obeying parents is hard and feels unjust. Also of note, this requirement is not based on whether or not the parents are believers. Children are called to conduct themselves at all times in a Christ-honoring way because *"this is right."*

In verse 2, Paul quoted the fifth of the Ten Commandments

(Deut. 5:16) when he declared, *"Honor your father and mother."* Honoring takes obedience to a whole new and higher level. He also reinforced the need to honor by emphasizing the *"promise"* tucked within this commandment.

Verse 3 goes on to quote this promise, *"... so that it may go well with you and that you may enjoy long life on the earth."* Some might argue that people who live obedient lives as children get their lives cut short all the time. The original commandment never calls this a *"promise"* per se, but indicates God's blessing on those who honor and obey their parents. Furthermore, we are not to question what God's blessings ultimately look like or involve. Besides, this promise is not the primary motivation given here, but only *the icing on the cake,* so to speak, for obeying our parents.

I find it intriguing how *"fathers"* are the ones singled out, in verse 4, and not *both* parents. Ironically, my father was the more self-controlled and mild-mannered of my two parents. But Paul probably focused on fathers, since they are the *"head"* of each family; thus, *the buck would stop with them.* But in my opinion *both* parents should follow this principle—striving not to *"exasperate"* our children. The Greek translation of this word is *"to provoke to anger."* I believe this means we should lead our children in ways that are fair and kind—*never abusive, neglectful or reckless.*

Paul then urged fathers to *"bring them up in the training and instruction of the Lord."* As believers, we can never take the view that our children don't need our godly and biblical instruction until they are teens or adults. It's important to teach them the truths of Scripture all throughout their childhoods and beyond. This reminds me of Deuteronomy 11:19, *"Teach them to your children, talking about them when you sit at home and when you walk along the road, when you lie down and when you get up."* Believing parents must take a daily and active role in guiding their children to love and obey the Lord.

Thought to take:
The first takeaway from this passage is for children to obey and honor their parents. However, since I am no longer a child and my parents are both deceased, I will focus on the second takeaway from this reading. Even though the second focus of being an encourager, rather than discourager of our children is *directed at fathers*, mother's can also aim for this high calling as well. As a parent, I want to always share with my children—*no matter their age*—the truths that God is teaching me, as well as living out God's truths before them in my life. So I will endeavor to keep this as my priority and practice each day. *(If you do not have children, this could be applied more generally—focusing on being a spiritual influencer.)*

T2t: Encourage spiritual growth in others

Help: Pray for God's help to apply your T2t both now and all day long.

Father, I realize that families of believers are great points of influence in our world. So may I do my best to encourage my children to live for You. I also commit to honoring those that You have placed in authority over me—knowing that this too draws others to You and Your love. Help me to influence others to obey You. And help them to trust that You will reward their attitudes and actions with all sorts of spiritual blessings and joys. Help me to also be sensitive and understanding of my children, so that I can avoid controlling or provoking them to anger. May I be found faithful in this task—constantly living out Your truths before my family, as well as before a watching world. In Jesus' name, amen.

Yield: Surrender yourself to God and His truths—reflecting on and applying your T2t all day long.

44 - CHAINS OF GRACE

Week 9, Day 4—Ephesians 6:5-6

Welcome the Lord: Ask Him to reveal His truth to you as you study.

Observe what the Scripture says:
5 - *Slaves, obey your earthly masters with respect and fear, and with sincerity of heart, just as you would obey Christ.*
6 - *Obey them not only to win their favor when their eye is on you, but as slaves of Christ, doing the will of God from your heart.*

Recognize what is noteworthy and true:
This passage might sound like an endorsement of slavery, but that's not what is truly being communicated here. It was simply the Apostle Paul's desire to guide believers who were slaves into right and godly actions. Biblical scholar C. F. D. Moule believed that the Gospel teachings—*though never directly protesting slavery*—undermined slavery through the revolutionary equality found in and through Christ. Moule said, "*So while the Gospel in one respect left slavery alone, it doomed it in another.*" It seems to me that God does not typically free believers from the harsh authority figures in our lives, but rather empowers us to rely on the ultimate and most gracious Authority in our lives—*Jesus Christ.*

In verse 5, Paul directed Christian slaves to *"obey"* their earthly masters—doing so with *"respect and fear,"* as well as *"with sincerity of heart."* He also told them to do these humble acts just like they humbly obey their Savior and Lord. First of all, the Greek meaning behind *"obey"* in this verse is to *"listen and attend"* their slave masters. But this command could also be applied to all authority figures and employers in our lives —*listening and attending* to their direction and needs. The slave is to do this with *"respect and fear,"* which is better translated, *"panic"* and *"trembling."* This seems to indicate a fear that *goes further than respect.* It might have been spoken this way to *reflect* the kind of fear and trembling we should have for the Lord when we are convinced of *His mighty power.* The idea behind the Greek translation of *"sincerity of heart"* is to have a single-minded focus—meaning we should *place our entire focus on Christ* when responding to our masters and leaders in life.

In verse 6, I notice that Paul assumed that these believing slaves would naturally try to win the favor of their masters. After all, there's nothing wrong with trying to please our bosses and leaders in life. But Paul also addressed the temptation to only please our masters *"when their eyes are on you."* This goes against the command to obey out of *"sincerity of heart"* (v. 5), since that would be serving and obeying out of what's in it for you, rather than out of a desire to honor Christ. Even though Christ has set believers free through His salvation, our redemption requires laying down *our lives for Christ's sake.* That makes us slaves to Jesus' grace. But that's exactly what I want to be chained to everyday—*God's grace.* So as a believer, I must let my gratitude for *Christ's love and forgiveness* be what drives me to humbly submit to the authority figures in my life. It is then that I am able to do the *"will of God"* and draw others to the paradoxical and mysterious *chains of grace.*

Thought to take:
This reading reminds me to obey the authority figures in my life out of the gratitude I feel for Christ's gift of grace and forgiveness to me. But I also see an important result of my obedience to the authority figures in my life—*which includes my husband, my pastor, law enforcement, and even the leaders of my government, etc.*

It shows that I'm ultimately obeying, honoring and fearing my Lord, whenever I do. I certainly want that to be what others see in my life! So I will keep Christ as my focus for obeying others—*chaining myself to His grace*—especially when I'm tempted today to resist other people's authority in my life.

T2t: Yield my will for Jesus' sake

Help: Pray for God's help to apply your T2t both now and all day long.

Father, this reading convinces me that humility and submission are such cornerstone commandments—*reflecting Christ's servant-hearted leadership and sacrifice.* So let me never stray from this realization. And encourage my heart at every turn to choose to respect and fear those You have put in authority over me. I want to do this out of sincerity of heart. For whenever I respect and fear my leaders in life, I'm ultimately doing so unto You. May You gain the glory whenever I humbly yield and unselfishly devote myself to them. The world stands up and takes notice of such mystifying and godly attitudes and actions—especially when the leaders in my life grow harsh and treat me unfairly. Use these moments to stretch my faith in Your mighty power—believing You never leave my side, nor let these situations spin out of Your redemptive control. I also thank You for freeing me from my sin and binding me to Your heart with the chains of grace. Let my life give evidence that I am completely and utterly Yours. In Jesus' name, amen.

Yield: Surrender yourself to God and His truths—reflecting on and applying your T2t all day long.

45 - HONOR THE TRUE MASTER

Week 9, Day 5—Ephesians 6:7-9

Welcome the Lord: Ask Him to reveal His truth to you as you study.

Observe what the Scripture says:

7 - *Serve wholeheartedly, as if you were serving the Lord, not people,*
8 - *because you know that the Lord will reward each one for what-ever good they do, whether they are slave or free.*
9 - *And masters, treat your slaves in the same way. Do not threaten them, since you know that he who is both their Master and yours is in heaven, and there is no favoritism with him.*

Recognize what is noteworthy and true:

Even though Paul was speaking directly to believers who were slaves in this passage *(and the one before)*, it is clear to me that verse 7 is a calling for *every believer*. As a Christ-follower, I have a *blessed duty* to serve every authority figure in my life *wholeheartedly*. Interestingly, the word *"wholeheartedly"* (used in the NIV) is actually better translated *"good will"* in the Greek. Certainly, possessing *"good will"* toward others includes the idea of serving wholeheartedly as well. Most importantly, when we serve wholeheartedly, it is actually the Christ-follower's way of serving the Lord, *not just people*. This is easy to lose sight of in the day-to-day, grind of life.

Verse 8 provides a promise from God—giving each believer a

"reward ... for whatever good they do." Paul also felt it necessary to say that this promise is not only for slaves, but also for those who are *"free"* or not enslaved. The reward of the Lord may not come as we expect or desire, but you can count on it being the *best reward.* God's ways are higher than ours, and He sees what we truly need so much better than we do. And though this promised reward gives us motivation to act in good and servant-hearted ways with others, it should never trump the primary goal and motivation of *serving the Lord.* For serving the Lord, is a reward in and of itself—*blessing us much more than any earthly or temporary blessing can or will.* I also think the emphasis of verse 8 is on how faithful and good our God is—never missing the chance to bless the good deeds we do in His name.

Paul turned his focus from believers who are slaves, to believing *masters* in verse 9. They are to treat their slaves in the same way that God treats us who are slaves of Christ (v. 6). It seems incongruous to me that a master would continue to hold slaves after coming to Christ. But often the transformation a believer undergoes takes time, *though it could emerge quickly as well.* The point here, in verse 9, is for masters—*or any authority figure in life*—to avoid using intimidation in their leadership. Christ-following slaveholders also needed to humbly remember that God is (was) *their* Master, as well as the Master of their slaves. The wonderful news is: *every Christ-follower is equally loved, accepted and valued by God!* Since this is the case, we should be careful to avoid showing favoritism in any of our relationships. Since leaders often wield great power, *the temptation to show favoritism must rise up almost constantly.* Yet, as believers, our focus should always be on honoring Christ in every possible way.

Thought to take:
No matter whether I am the one in authority or the one under someone else's authority, I need to always choose to be submissive and humble. So as I go about this day, I will focus on real-

izing that every act of good I do and obedience I show to my authority figures honors and blesses the Lord. It is to Him that I am ultimately serving and obeying. Whenever I keep Him as my primary focus, I know that I will find the motivation I need to persevere in being humble and devoted—*no matter the actions or choices of my authority figures.*

T2t: Serve my leaders gladly as unto the Lord

Help: Pray for God's help to apply your T2t both now and all day long.

Father, there is much work that I need to do in order to serve You wholeheartedly. So open my eyes to see all the ways I need to conform myself to Christ's servant-hearted example. I want You to know without a doubt that I am choosing You every time I obey, respect and honor those You have put in authority over me. I want my devotion to You to shine clearly through these moments of surrender—*drawing others to You, my mysterious and marvelous Master.* I thank You for providing blessings for the good that I do, which only further reminds me of what a good and attentive Father You are. I also pray that I would remember to treat everyone with the same acceptance and equality that You continually show—*never resorting to intimidation or threats to try and control others.* Help me to win their hearts for You! I commit to accept and serve them, as well as being gentle with others in every way possible. In Jesus' name, amen.

Yield: Surrender yourself to God and His truths—reflecting on and applying your T2t all day long.

Week Nine Group Discussion Questions

5:28-30—A 'One Body' Kind of Love

What are some specific needs of your spouse *(or others, if you're single)* that you want to pay more attention to and meet? What hinders you from keeping Christ's caring example in mind when meeting other people's needs?

5:31-33—One Plus One is One

What are some unloving and disrespectful actions/attitudes we tend to do in our lives and/or marriages that do not reflect the oneness we experience in Christ's body?

6:1-4—A Family that Honors God

What is one thing you could do to improve how you honor the authority figures in your life? How can you avoid exasperating your children or others that you are endeavoring to spiritually lead?

6:5-6—Chains of Grace

What types of authority figures in your life do you struggle to respect and sincerely follow, and why? How can you show them greater respect, fear, and/or sincerity?

6:7-9—Honor the True Master

What are some ways to honor our true Master—*the Lord*—in how we relate to authority figures? How can you best honor the Lord with those you lead and influence?

46 - POWER TO FIGHT
THE REAL ENEMY

Week 10, Day 1—Ephesians 6:10-12

Welcome the Lord: Ask Him to reveal His truth to you as you study.

Observe what the Scripture says:
10 - Finally, be strong in the Lord and in his mighty power.
11 - Put on the full armor of God, so that you can take your stand against the devil's schemes.
12 - For our struggle is not against flesh and blood, but against the rulers, against the authorities, against the powers of this dark world and against the spiritual forces of evil in the heavenly realms.

Recognize what is noteworthy and true:
Paul concluded his letter and chapter with one of the most profound and impacting messages in the Bible in verse 10. This verse alone brings such encouragement to my heart, since I'm facing a daunting season in my life with a difficult day ahead. But as I come to this reading, Paul's words reach from almost two thousand years ago to today—*lifting my spirit and reminding me of the infinite strength found in God's mighty power.* And God does not hoard His power like so many authority figures in life might try to do. He wants to fill up every weak corner in my heart and life with His boundless power. The question then becomes: *Will I seek Him and receive the gift of His power that He constantly extends?*

In verse 11, Paul jumped right in to unpack the practical side of receiving God's mighty power, saying believers must *"put on the full armor of God."* No soldier would leave off a piece of his armor when going out to battle, *unless he was on a suicide mission.* As believers, we face battles every day, some days unexpectedly fiercer than others. So we must be sure to put on every piece of God's armor as we go into the fray. One reason we put on our armor is so that we can *"stand against the devil's schemes."* It's important to remember that demonic forces are active in the spiritual realm in ways that we cannot see; yet we must recognize they are very real and present each day. Without the full armor of God we become like *sitting ducks—perfect targets of their crafty and invisible strategies.*

In verse 12, Paul reminds us *"our struggle is not against flesh and blood."* I tend to assume that the conflicts and struggles I face are due in large part to the people in my life. And though there are people who do stir up trouble, I need to remember that the enemy may be as much or *more responsible* for my troubles than humans are in life. When I remain focused on others, it's like a soldier taking his sword and turning it on his comrade in arms. But when I realize and assume that the enemy is likely behind much of my problem, I'm free to fight back darkness, instead of letting anger darken my heart. Blaming others can be set aside in favor of proactive and preemptive measures.

Paul went on to list several types of demonic forces in verse 12. It sounds almost like there is some type of hierarchy, since there are: rulers, authorities, powers of this dark world, and spiritual forces of evil listed here. Whether there's actually a hierarchy among the demons or not, they all have one unified purpose—*to discourage and trap the believer in sin.* They are the true enemies in our lives; but we are able to wield God's mighty power—*making them no match against our God.*

Thought to take:
I see from this reading the need to recognize that there are many spiritual forces of evil in the world that I cannot see, yet are all

around me. I don't want to recognize this out of fear, but out of the need to be vigilant against my real enemies in this life, instead of getting angry with other humans, who are often used like pawns of the enemy. So I will choose to strengthen myself in the Lord and His mighty power whenever conflicts, temptations and troubles come my way—letting my every thought, feeling and action be empowered by and focused on Christ alone.

T2t: Rely on Jesus' power in my struggles

Help: Pray for God's help to apply your T2t both now and all day long.

Father, if there is anything that I can glean and apply from this powerful letter, it is to be strong in Your mighty power. I want to avoid putting any confidence in my own strength or wit, but fully look to You for strength. Help me to put on each piece of armor—knowing that every day brings a spiritual battle in my life. The enemy is crafty, scheming and relentless; but You, O Lord, outwit him every time—*having already won the war through Christ!* For I know that Jesus gives me *His* armor—the armor He wore into the battle to beat all battles. So if Christ's armor was enough for Him to be victorious, then I know it is more than enough for the battles I face. Keep me always conscious of the fact that it is often the spiritual forces of evil that trip me and others up, so that I do not fall for the devil's trick of *"the blame game."* Enable me to turn my fears into prayers that lift up others, as well as myself when the battle grows fierce. Thank You for securing the victory for me! In Jesus' name, amen.

Yield: Surrender yourself to God and His truths—reflecting on and applying your T2t all day long.

47 - WEARING OUR 'ARMOR' WELL

Week 10, Day 2—*Ephesians 6:13-15*

Welcome the Lord: Ask Him to reveal His truth to you as you study.

Observe what the Scripture says:

13 - *Therefore put on the full armor of God, so that when the day of evil comes, you may be able to stand your ground, and after you have done everything, to stand.*

14 - *Stand firm then, with the belt of truth buckled around your waist, with the breastplate of righteousness in place,*

15 - *and with your feet fitted with the readiness that comes from the gospel of peace.*

Recognize what is noteworthy and true:

In verse 13, Paul repeated his command from verse 11, re-stating the need to put on the *"full armor of God."* The reason we must put on the full armor of God is *"so that when the day of evil comes, you may be able to stand your ground ..."* The first mention of *"stand"* is actually better translated *"withstand"* or *"resist."* The second mention of *"stand"* is best understood as *planting ourselves firmly in and on God and His word.* The first idea involves action and *even movement* against evil and toward God, while the second involves remaining *unmoved* in the power, truth and security of God. Therefore, the idea of having *"done everything"* involves following these two directives—*moving against spirit-*

ual forces of evil and standing firmly with and in the Lord.

In verse 14, Paul began to detail what soldiers of God should wear for their armor in every spiritual battle. He first talked about how the *"belt of truth"* must be *buckled* around our waist in order for us to stand firm in our faith. This metaphor mirrors the belt that soldiers at this time would have worn. The belt was not something that directly protected a soldier, but instead gathered the pieces together and held them in place as an essential connection piece of protection. The truth of God's word holds together all that we feel, think, do and say as Christ-followers. God's truth must be central to our faith—giving us the ability to fight spiritual battles effectively and without hindrances.

Paul then mentioned how the *"breastplate of righteousness"* needs to be *"in place,"* which would have provided essential protection to the vital organs of a soldier. First of all, this righteousness reflects the righteous position that a believer gains through faith in Christ alone. Secondly, it also must refer to the righteous acts or practical holiness we pursue through our godly conduct and character. These aspects of our righteousness go hand-in-hand and allow us to reflect Christ's righteousness, rather than self-righteousness, which is rooted in our own human accomplishments.

The apostle went on, in verse 15, to mention the need to have our *"feet fitted with the readiness that comes from the gospel of peace."* The soldiers in this day and age wore shoes with spikes that helped them to run fast and firmly toward their enemies. In a sense, we gain traction through the gospel of peace, because the gospel of Christ brings peace to every heart that receives His transformative truth and salvation. Since every day brings a spiritual battle of one degree or another, I must prepare my heart with the gospel of peace so that I can run confidently into the fray.

Thought to take:

I see three important applications and focuses to take today:

buckling the belt of truth, keeping the breastplate of righteousness in place, and wearing shoes shod with the gospel of peace. When I apply and live out these three main focuses, I am able to withstand evil and stand firmly in the Lord. So I will ground myself in God's word and truth. I will live out His truths so that His righteous character is demonstrated in and through my life. And I will then let His peace bring calmness and confidence to every anxiety I might feel, especially when the spiritual battle grows fierce.

T2t: Rely on God's truth, righteousness, peace

Help: Pray for God's help to apply your T2t both now and all day long.

Father, this passage is a rallying cry to prepare myself for the battle that constantly wages in ways that I often do not see. So give me the motivation and commitment to put on all the pieces of Your armor each day. For I know this will allow me to stand *against* evil and *for* Your good. I commit to securing the belt of Your truth—knowing Your truth keeps all the other pieces of my armor in place. So I commit myself to study and then apply Your truths in every battle I face today. I also want to remember how Your Son has given me His righteousness. But let me never become so complacent in that amazing gift that I do not furiously run toward holiness and righteousness in my character and conduct as well. This effort will not only protect my heart in times of battle, but protect my witness for You as well. Finally, I commit to wearing the gospel of peace, especially when I feel threatened and afraid. So in tense moments, I will reach for Your peace—going on to extend the gospel of peace to all that I meet as well. In Christ's name, amen.

Yield: Surrender yourself to God and His truths—reflecting on and applying your T2t all day long.

48 - EXTINGUISH AND IGNITE

Week 10, Day 3—Ephesians 6:16-18a

Welcome the Lord: Ask Him to reveal His truth to you as you study.

Observe what the Scripture says:

16 - *In addition to all this, take up the shield of faith, with which you can extinguish all the flaming arrows of the evil one.*

17 - *Take the helmet of salvation and the sword of the Spirit, which is the word of God.*

18a - *And pray in the Spirit on all occasions with all kinds of prayers and requests.*

Recognize what is noteworthy and true:

Paul moved from one type of armor of the Lord to another type, here in verse 16—moving from what we *"put on"* (vv. 14-15) to what we should *"take up,"* which is *"the shield of faith."* Maybe the reason for the difference is that the previous aspects of our armor are all pieces we must *constantly* wear, while the shield of faith, helmet of salvation (v. 17), and sword of the Spirit (v. 17) are all aspects readily available, and must be taken up and wielded as the need arises. Apparently there were two types of shields used by warriors back in this day and time. The type that Paul referenced here points to the larger of the two shields. This type of shield was driven into the ground to form something as protective as a door—*shielding the entire body.*

Further on in verse 16, Paul gave the reason why we need to *take up* the shield of faith. It is to *"extinguish all the flaming arrows of the evil one."* There's something unique and corollary to this illustration. We feel the enemy's arrows piercing our hearts with temptation and/or trials, but the pain and destruction only worsen as the fiery dart begins to burn and consume us. Our hope against being hit by these nasty darts of the devil is to extinguish them with *our faith* in the Lord.

In verse 17, Paul directed us to *"take the helmet of salvation."* In 1 Thessalonians 5:8, Paul referred to this helmet as the *"hope of salvation,"* so this reference here is likely to our constant hope and trust in the salvation that is already in place in a believer's life. This is probably one of the most effective ways that the enemy can defeat us—by tempting us to question our faith, as well as the power of our Lord to save and keep us saved. Moving further in this verse, we are told to take the *"sword of the Spirit, which is the word of God."* This is the first and only *weapon* mentioned. All the other items are defensive. This reminds me of just how powerful and convicting God's word is. When I am familiar with how to wield my sword—*the word of God*—I am able to slay the forces of evil that stand in my way each day. But if I am not familiar with my sword, it is useless to me or can even become a hindrance.

In verse 18a, Paul wrapped up his listing of the armor of God with a call to *"pray in the Spirit."* I notice that prayer was not correlated with a specific piece of the armor. This might be because prayer is almost always unseen by our enemies. It's like a *secret weapon* that can be utilized in the heat of battle—beckoning our Lord to fight fiercely for us. I also note that we must *"do this on all occasions and with all kinds of prayers and requests."* This reminds me of the importance of staying in constant contact with the Commander of the Lord's army so that I can follow His orders at every turn.

Thought to take:

I see two main pieces of armor from this reading to take up in my day. The first involves taking up my *faith in God* and the second is taking up my *hope in His salvation* of my soul. These are both ways to extinguish the enemy's darts that can result in discouragement, distraction and destruction in my life, and provide refreshing encouragement in the Lord and His power. So as I go about my day, I will prayerfully ignite my faith in God, as well as prayerfully extinguishing any doubts and fears I have with a firm hope and trust in Christ's sure and unalterable salvation of my life.

T2t: Extinguish fear by igniting faith and hope

Help: Pray for God's help to apply your T2t both now and all day long.

Father, these are direct orders from You, my true and only Commander! They make me want to be a skilled and ready soldier in Your army. Empower me to prayerfully take up the shield of my faith, so that I can extinguish the flaming arrows of the evil one. When my faith grows weak, remind me of the hope and certainty of my salvation—using this to encourage me in every battle I go through today. I also commit to the serious study and application of Your word. For I know that a soldier who does not know how to wield his sword is a handicap to the rest of Your army. I'm also committed to praying all throughout my day to ignite my faith and hope in You, so that I can extinguish every fear. This secret weapon not only pushes back the evil forces in my life, but it brings greater clarity and comfort to my heart when I need it most. Thank You for providing everything I need to prevail in Your power. In Jesus' name, amen.

Yield: Surrender yourself to God and His truths—reflecting on and applying your T2t all day long.

49 - WE'RE ALL IN NEED
OF PRAYER

Week 10, Day 4—Ephesians 6:18b-20

Welcome the Lord: Ask Him to reveal His truth to you as you study.

Observe what the Scripture says:
18b - *With this in mind, be alert and always keep on praying for all the Lord's people.*
19 - *Pray also for me, that whenever I speak, words may be given so that I will fearlessly make known the mystery of the gospel,*
20 - *for which I am an ambassador in chains. Pray that I may declare it fearlessly, as I should.*

Recognize what is noteworthy and true:
It is clear from this reading that I need to reflect back on what Paul had in mind in the early part of this verse (v. 18a) so that I can know what to *keep in my mind* here today. It makes sense in verse 18b that Paul wanted believers to bear in mind the need to be *"alert"* and vigilant in our prayers. The actual Greek translation of *"alert"* is to *"be sleepless."* Whenever I have a case of insomnia, more times than not, it's because my mind has latched onto some issue that I cannot shake. In the same way, God wants us to be so consumed with praying that it invades our every thought and action.

Paul's mention of praying *"on all occasions"* (v. 18a) was reiterated here (v. 18b) when he said that we must *"keep on"* praying. This makes it clear that we should never cease our intimate and often internal dialogue with the Lord. Paul then directed believers to focus these continual prayers on *"all the Lord's people."* It's easy to forget the need to lift other believers up in prayer with all the busyness and demands of life. However, since we form the family of God, we need to love our brothers and sisters in Christ through our ongoing and continual prayer support for them.

In verse 19, Paul showed his vulnerable side—*something he often revealed in all of his letters*—by requesting prayer support for *himself*. He wanted them to pray for him to be able to *"fearlessly make known the mystery of the gospel ..."* Paul could have asked for so many other requests at this time—*being released from his chains (v. 20), for one*. Yet his main concern and desire for prayer had to do with being able to fearlessly or boldly proclaim the *"mystery of the gospel."* It's important to realize that he might have had in mind his impending appearance and defense before Caesar—hoping to proclaim the gospel in that public, *but also intimidating*, forum.

In verse 20, Paul's reference to being an *"ambassador in chains"* sounds like he felt grateful, even privileged, to represent Christ. Surely, if he had in mind his future appearance before Caesar when making this request, he would have known how mysterious and, *quite frankly, strange* the gospel message would seem to this powerful emperor and the others present. Perhaps that figured into his request—giving evidence that he might have struggled with fears about this task. *What normal human wouldn't struggle in this way?* Yet Paul never shrunk back from his calling of boldly declaring the gospel—knowing what was always at stake for himself, as well as for every listener.

Thought to take:

I recognize the need to be vigilant and continual in my prayers, as well as alert to the needs of my brothers and sisters in Christ. So I will make it my aim today to discover all the ways that my believing friends need prayer—*focusing particularly on their spiritual needs and challenges.* I will also follow Paul's example and vulnerably share my prayer requests with my godly friends, seeking their prayer support as well. I will remain committed to praying all day long—not stopping in this effort until my head hits the pillow tonight.

T2t: Seek prayer, while lifting others up as well

Help: Pray for God's help to apply your T2t both now and all day long.

Father, I want to always keep in mind the need for ongoing and vigilant prayer—*not just for myself, but also for my brothers and sisters in Christ.* For I realize that we are under far more spiritual attacks in life than we can ever see or realize. Allow me to attune my mind to recognize when I am being spiritually attacked, as well as staying alert to these needs in my godly friends' lives. I commit to pray for their needs in this way and will seek to be vulnerable about my own struggles and needs with them as well—requesting their prayer support in turn. I never want to lose sight of what is at stake each day. So fuel my desire to live boldly and fearlessly for You. Give me opportunities to share my faith and live out Your gospel; because I know how blessed I am to be an ambassador of Your gospel demonstrated through my godly and persevering actions each day. In Jesus' name, amen.

Yield: Surrender yourself to God and His truths—reflecting on and applying your T2t all day long.

50 - ENCOURAGEMENTS FOR ALL

Week 10, Day 5—Ephesians 6:21-24

Welcome the Lord: Ask Him to reveal His truth to you as you study.

Observe what the Scripture says:

21 - *Tychicus, the dear brother and faithful servant in the Lord, will tell you everything, so that you also may know how I am and what I am doing.*

22 - *I am sending him to you for this very purpose, that you may know how we are, and that he may encourage you.*

23 - *Peace to the brothers and sisters, and love with faith from God the Father and the Lord Jesus Christ.*

24 - *Grace to all who love our Lord Jesus Christ with an undying love.*

Recognize what is noteworthy and true:

The first thing that catches my eye here, in verse 21, is the unusual name of *"Tychicus,"* the man Paul referred to here as *"the dear brother and faithful servant in the Lord."* Apparently this faithful servant had been a long time friend of Paul's—serving the churches throughout the region in a variety of ways. Not only was Tychicus being utilized as a messenger, but he also ministered in other ways as well, like occasionally serving as a temporary pastor for each of Timothy and Titus' respective churches. His task on this occasion was to go and tell the Ephesians *"everything"* about Paul so that they would know how their beloved apostle was faring and all that he was doing while under arrest.

In verse 22, Paul explained more thoroughly his motive for sending Tychicus. Paul wanted to reassure these believers of how and what he was doing, so that *they would be encouraged.* After all, Paul surely knew his days were numbered; yet Paul's main concern was for the welfare of these people. He only wanted to encourage *them* in *their* faith, rather than focus on his own uncomfortable and dire circumstances. Of course, communication between believers must have been so difficult and dangerous at this time in history. This gives evidence of Tychicus' bold faith in God as well—being willing to brave every danger and obstacle in order to get this important message to the people.

In verses 23-24, Paul drew his letter to a close by sending the same prayer and sentiment that he began his letter with —*"peace"* and *"grace"* (Eph. 1:2)—to his *"brothers and sisters"* in Christ. He added one more focus to his prayerful hope for these people, wishing them *"love with faith."* This echoes Paul's words in Galatians 5:6b, *"The only thing that counts is faith expressing itself through love."* So it seems that Christ's love can only be extended and empowered in our hearts when we love *through faith in God.* Every human being has experienced the challenge of loving those who act in unloving or even hateful ways. In those challenging moments the only way we can truly love others is by relying *in faith* on Christ to love mightily *through us* to those who hurt and hate us back.

Paul's final words in verse 24 describe another motivator for loving others through our faith in Christ. Our love rises out of the love we feel for Christ. Paul described it here as an *"undying love."* For me, that means loving others in a way that never gives up. It means letting Christ's love flow through me and *resurrecting* the love that felt dead and gone, so that I can love others in *miraculous and divinely inspired ways.*

Thought to take:

This reading inspires me to model both Paul and Tychicus' brave faith and selfless devotion to others. I want to set about each day to focus more completely on encouraging *others*, rather than focusing on being encouraged, though I will surely seek that from my godly friends when I am in need. Most of all, I want to receive my encouragement from the *Lord*, so that I can remain a strong and constant encourager in the lives of others. All of this can only be achieved through my faith activating and extending Christ's *love* to others.

T2t: Love and encourage through faith in Christ

Help: Pray for God's help to apply your T2t both now and all day long.

Father, I am so grateful for the faithful men and women who bravely served in every possible way under all sorts of challenging circumstances—*giving hope and faith to the people in the early church and beyond*. Their unselfish and unswerving devotion is so inspiring to me. It motivates me to respond in those same godly and sacrificial ways with others in my life—in particular with the body of Christ. Empower me for that task this day. Make encouraging others my priority and focus, using it to encourage my own heart in the day-to-day challenges of this life. I also pray that I would focus on the peace, grace and love that You offer in abundance to me each and every day. Help me to activate my faith in Your undying love so that my actions of love come straight from Your heart to every love-hungry person in my life. Use this to encourage them in deeply spiritual ways. In Jesus' name, amen.

Yield: Surrender yourself to God and His truths—reflecting on and applying your T2t all day long.

Week Ten Group Discussion Questions

6:10-12—Power to Fight the Real Enemy

How often do you stop and realize, in times of conflict, that your real enemy is Satan? What are some ways you can shift your focus from blaming and fighting against others, to putting on God's armor?

6:13-15—Wearing Our 'Armor' Well

Which of these pieces of armor—God's truth, Godly conduct, His peace—do you need to work on securing more in your life? How can you do that?

6:16-18a—Extinguish and Ignite

Which of these aspects of the armor of God—faith, salvation, word of God, prayer—do you need to strengthen the most in your life? How can you do this?

6:18b-20—We're All in Need of Prayer

What is one way you need another Christ-follower to pray for you today? *Then be sure to pray for each other at the end of your Bible study time today!*

6:21-24—Encouragements for All

Who are some people in your life that need extra encouragement and a sense that you feel undying love for them? What are some ways you can show this to them?